LOOKING AT YO

A MESSAGE FOR THE BROKEN HEARTED

THE TERRIBLE VOICE OF SATAN

LAZY BRIEN

Gregory Motton

PLAYS TWO

LOOKING AT YOU (REVIVED) AGAIN

A MESSAGE FOR THE BROKEN HEARTED

THE TERRIBLE VOICE OF SATAN

LAZY BRIEN

OBERON BOOKS
LONDON

First published in this collection in 1998
by Oberon Books Ltd. (incorporating Absolute Classics)
521 Caledonian Road, London N7 9RH
Tel: 0171 607 3637 / Fax: 0171 607 3629

Looking at You (revived) Again first published by Methuen in 1989

A Message for the Broken Hearted and *The Terrible Voice of Satan* first
published by Flood Books, 1995

Gregory Motton is hereby identified as author of these works
in accordance with section 77 of the Copyright, Designs and
Patents Act 1988. The author has asserted his moral rights.

All rights whatsoever in these plays are strictly reserved
and application for performance etc. should be made before
commencement of rehearsals to Gregory Motton c/o Oberon
Books Ltd. at the above address.

British Library Cataloguing-in-Publication Data
A catalogue record for this book is available from the British
Library.

ISBN 1 84002 020 2

Cover design: Andrzej Klimowski

Typography: Richard Doust

Printed in Great Britain by Antony Rowe Ltd., Reading.

CONTENTS

INTRODUCTION

Gregory Motton enjoyed a brief period of theatrical fashion in the mid to late eighties when several of his plays were performed at the Royal Court Theatre. However the New Plays establishment misunderstood the nature of these plays. The marketing people promoted him principally as a chronicler of urban decline under Thatcher. I remember someone at the Royal Court saying: 'He's read nothing, you know. Well, I think he might have read a little Oscar Wilde.' They briefly condescended to inspect his gutter, but the firmament above his head was richer and subtler than they imagined. The New Writing authorities have been edging him towards the mad pile ever since; a place where I've no doubt the likes of Pinter's *No Man's Land* would end up if received unsolicited now. Motton won't be the first playwright to grow in importance as his plays cease to be performed. Like one of Strindberg's night flowers he has enlarged his canvas, unnoticed, beyond what has been attempted for many years. Or rather he has been noticed because one's view of the author of these plays is a very defining thing in theatre circles today; not that anyone would admit it. The silence is deafening.

Motton's range was apparent in his earliest produced plays, *Chicken, Ambulance* and *Downfall.* They were comments, certainly, on the time, but they didn't fetishise it as less canny writers do. Seeing some plays nowadays is like going to a meeting, they're designed to keep terror at bay. What struck me about Motton's plays was how personal they were; so personal that you could see under their skin, connect with them only painfully. They weren't mostly general and a little personal like most plays of the time; this was real life and it needed a special tension in the language to pour through. Emily Dickinson advises: 'Tell all the Truth – but tell it Slant.' Motton had a Slant, which is rare in the theatre. You knew at once that you'd always recognise any line from one of his plays. He was a modernist in a form not overburdened with them. Sir Richard Eyre was recently quoted as saying: 'The great thing about the theatre is that modernism can't touch it.' In fact what modernism has done is force the medium much closer to life as we really experience it. Strindberg, O'Neill, Becket, these are Motton's precursors. Beckett once said to an actor who found a line of his incomprehensible: 'You've been saying it all your life.' A director of Motton's plays might well want to give this advice as well.

> 'Look at the place. I'm so untidy. I can never remember anything. And I eat rubbish. And I've got such a fierce temper. How would I have shouted at you. My eyes are rat's eyes. Rat's eyes.' (Ellis in *Ambulance*)

Motton's plays are unashamedly real and sharply lyrical in the same instant. This was clear from the beginning. But he's developed some new dimensions to his writing over the years. He could always give two and more sides in a sexual relationship; but where we once found God in old plays he inserts the unconscious as a fully fledged dramatic tool, rather than just an analogue to character and action.

These developments allied to an ever greater economy in his slant manner yielded *Looking at You (revived) Again*, the first play in this volume. Set in the semi-rural shadow of North London, which for Motton begins somewhere around King's Cross, and its gloomy environs, this, like *Waiting for Godot*, is the story of a marriage; as well as time, distance, and the psyche. Abe, an Irishman from a line of smallholders exiled in England, is the shirker-adventurer who drifts between his crippled wife and a young girl, P.D. (Peragrin's Daughter) while searching for his lost children. He roves a world of soaring emotion revolving in a poisoned well, a shadow universe in which the three characters are far adrift from their original selves as well as being, agonisingly, parts of each other. They can be any number of other people as well, 'all the dead voices' in Beckett's words. Sometimes, though, reality clears a little path for them, and it doesn't look good.

ABE: Oh, if they'd rolled the Earth as flat as they've rolled you and me, we'd have fallen off the edge of it long ago

DARK WOMAN: Go away from me now. You stink the stink of loneliness. You're desperate about every minute and every night, aren't you? Well, I'm not. I think of it year by year, and I've never fallen to my knees in the small hours in front of the mirror and asked – who, who, who will speak to me? –

The memory of love lies buried under a landslide of anger, bitterness and introversion, not to mention financial worry, alcohol and hypochondria. The play begins with a reenactment of Abe's wedding to the dark woman and ends with him begging for comfort from the wife he's deserted and a girl, possibly their daughter, who's just miscarried their baby.

Motton is a fine writer about London, and cities, and especially the loneliness and decay at the heart of them. Walk through King's Cross Station at three in the morning, and you will see and hear these characters. We also recognise in the plays our own grandiose moments, our baleful cries for help, our flat terror; to understand what they are for. And it is consoling and moral to do so. Abe is disintegrating. P.D. seems to possess the spontaneity and intoxication he needs; but each one is, tragically, the shadow of the other. Much of the play's dramatic strength lies in this irony.

P.D.: Do you love me?

ABE: Love?

P.D.: All men love me

ABE: You're mistaken...

P.D.: Abe

ABE: Ester, Ester, help me

P.D.: Who's that you're calling?

ABE: My wife. She did first aid I remember

The scenes place everyday details in a dream structure; a more familiar technique in poetry and fiction, but rare in contemporary theatre and very difficult to do; hard to realise as well. *Looking at You* requires a rhythmic precision in the playing beyond even the rigorous demands of his earliest plays, and yet at the same time its shifting emotions need to remain almost unarticulated.

Though at times lyrical and naturalistic with exquisitely painted moods – it could be Synge – the play is resolutely internal. The psychoanalyst DW Winnicott is illuminating here: "The chaos in the external world which is engineered by the (depressive patient) represents the individual's attempt to show what the inside is like. In defense against such a procedure the individual may become obsessed with the need for external orderly neurosis, as in obsessional neurosis, but obsessional behaviour all the time points to chaos within, so that the obsessively orderly neurosis cannot heal because it can only deal with external representations or denials of the inner chaos."

In *A Message for the Broken Hearted*, the persona of Abe is replaced by Mickey, a biker of sorts with fits of blindness when he staggers around panicking. He has two lovers and an unhealthy relationship with the father of one of them. Motton refines the dream idiom in this play, but his treatment of everyday life driven by neuroses – his comment on Beckett's marriages – is startingly real.

> LINDA: I just don't like it when you think I'm abnormal
>
> MICKEY: How do you know I think you're abnormal
>
> LINDA: Because I am. But if you were nice to me
> I'd be better.
>
> MICKEY: I am nice to you
>
> LINDA: Never for long enough
>
> MICKEY: Because you're never better for long enough

There are echoes of Kroetz and Fassbinder in the unflinching reproduction of what people actually do to one another in rooms and houses. But Motton is a writer of sharp contrasts and he rarely leaves a play in one place for long. As in life one thing ends and another begins, often without warning; in *Message* we move from troughs of daily neurosis and depression to fragments of Jacobean-size gesture.

MICKEY: What are you doing?

JENINE: I'm trying to wash my heart (*She gets up, her peace disturbed, drops the heart into the water.*) Why haven't you been to see me? You seem to be cooling off, that's never happened before. I suppose you're tired of it all. I am. Linda is. You must be

These characters are provocatively self-indulgent with child-like emotions; how else could they be in a late neurotic age when everyone is supposed to be tough and independent? Such heroism, tenderness and ability to trust as they possess can't exist. Nor can failure. Society has jettisoned any communal morality and yet all human weakness that drives us to our knees is punished without mercy. There are rights but there is no pity. Motton has grasped the moment we are living through in a moral and a psychological sense as well as a visceral sense; and he shows the toll a mean age extracts from anyone who is not prepared to sacrifice their humanity. His characters are weak for the most part, and they have long failed to function adequately in society's terms, but they can be heroic as well as perverse. The broken heart belongs to each one of them in *Message*; and to each one of us listening, watching, and waiting to break loose from this world into a better one.

They think I really do hear voices but that's just the way the wind tunes in like with a radio. I had a radio down by the rushes by the bridge, a stick like a divining rod, they'd given her to some Jews and they'd just left her, I had to look after her all by myself. There's something not quite right there isn't there? They put you into care and then they try and make you work for

> them. I said listen, if I want to I can take her to my
> mother so don't stand over me checking if I know what
> I'm doing because I do know, I know and I've done it
> all before. (Jenine in *A Message for the Broken Hearted*)

If you hesitate for a moment nowadays faced with life's difficulties, someone's telling you what to think, what to feel, what they think, how to fix it, who to call. We live in a neurotic tyranny. The characters in *Message* are violent and inward but they are not bullies, and in that may be a speck of salvation. Motton combines self and social satire in his personae to temper the hysteria which now threatens to overwhelm or paralyse all life. He is at least half a moralist and like any worth the name he makes things painfully difficult for himself. But the message he rescues is a testament to things felt and endured; the aim of a true satirist. The moral-satirical strand in Motton's writing led to the recent *Cat and Mouse (Sheep)*, a state of the nation play that begins where David Hare's nightmares end, and is perhaps the most important British play of its kind since *Look Back in Anger*.

Tom Doheny, Motton's next leading character, freewheels into the picaresque of *The Terrible Voice of Satan*, with his mother in a wheelbarrow.

TOM: Why don't you give us a song as we go

MA: I will not. I've sung my throat to ribbons over
    the Christmas festivities, I'm voiceless

TOM: A great quality in a mother

MA: Never you mind your qualities get some elbow
    into it. Oh why did we have to come on the boat,
    why didn't we fly over like decent people?

DA: The boat's fine

MA: Gee you're earthbound if ever a man was.
    Don't be earthbound like your father son.

In *Terrible Voice*, perhaps his funniest play, Motton threads his story of the Irish in exile through a fluid and ever-changing landscape of personal and social satire and makes it gripping. Yet still at its heart lie the daily domestic particulars which tie the tale down in all its cavorting range and breath; references to the tract of North London which is Motton's own, especially Archway, and little volleys of self-lacerating satire.

> TOM: I must leave you now and write a letter. The
>   hour prior to sleep is my best writing hour. I strap
>   myself to the mast of my pen while the waves of
>   my unconscious rise up about me. I awake in the
>   morning to see the inky measure of their wrath
>   on the page beside me
> PRIEST: Is it any wonder she despises you.
>   She wants a highway in the sand, you give
>   her shipwrecks from your pillow

The crippling hysteria, the terrible emptiness, are still present, still the reference; but the frieze of sorrow has dissolved a little as Motton allows his ironies room to do their worst. Like Abe and Mickey, Tom Doheny is a weak man, a clueless romantic; but where they were in part tragic characters, he is the ideal deadpan persona to transport us far into the heart of our eerie climate as the century ends, with its history of mass murder and, latterly, its near global institutional mendacity. Motton is the true playwright of this climate. I can think of no more accurate comment on the philosophy inferred by Motton's world of manifold ironies than these opening sentences from the Italian writer Natalia Ginzburg's essay *The Little Virtues*. Speaking of children, she says: 'They should be taught not the small virtues but the great ones. Not thrift but generosity and an indifference to money; not caution but courage and a contempt for danger; not shrewdness but frankness and a love of truth; not tact but love for one's neighbour and self-denial; nor a desire for success but a desire to be and to know.' Sadly, Nazism was a triumph of the very same pettiness which is seeping into our sick psyche once more; Motton extracts much comedy from this state of affairs but his message is urgent.

> HACKETT: My masturbation is a great source
>   of jealousy to my wife. As well it ought to be

> COOMEY: God I'm lonely

> HACKETT: Ha! There was a time when I would
>   have felt pity for you but nowadays everyone is
>   lonely, everyone is upset, but ask them why they
>   are upset and they can't tell you

For *Lazy Brien*, the sole radio play in this volume, Motton forsakes the bleak hills of London for a rural location in Ireland, the point of setting out for many of his characters. Caught between his mother's evil tongue and his wife's vast appetite, Brien ends up being swallowed alive by a goat. Part North European folk-tale, part yarn, the play unfolds in a gentle shadow world; yet through the shadows we can see who these people really are and how they really survive. It is *A Message for the Broken Hearted* by other means, a comedy about the selfishness and brutality of everyday life.

> I myself am my own devil, the antagonist who
> always wants the opposite to everything. Can we
> ever really endure ourselves?

> 'Do onto others...' This is as true of evil as of
> good... (C.G. Jung, *The Psychology of the Transference*)

Gregory Motton is a poet of our moment and our terrible future. He writes neither by subject, parallel, nor metaphor, he shows us how we're devouring ourselves and each other and urges us to change. He sets out neither to shock his audience nor to belittle anyone. Like the Brecht of *The Good Woman of Setzuan* or *St. Joan of the Stockyards* he knows that a small delicate instrument could in the right circumstances effect great change. The tyranny he identifies is one of neurosis, panic, bullying, fear and stupidity; the index of a world built on lies. His plays aren't obscure, there is a cry in them; they are potentially consoling and changing in a way that doesn't simply throw us back into the sickness. Like some Rabelaisian therapist he chokes up life's impossibility in order at last to make it possible, and in doing this he joins a fine tradition of rebels whose line stretches back far beyond the current theatre's brief memory span. You will have to read these plays for yourself as no description can do justice to their elusive surface or their sudden depth; but I for one believe him to be one of our major playwrights.

Simon Usher
London, 1997

LOOKING AT YOU (REVIVED) AGAIN

Characters

ABE

DARK WOMAN

PERAGRIN'S DAUGHTER

LOOKING AT YOU (REVIVED) AGAIN was first performed at the Haymarket Theatre, Leicester, in June 1989. It was directed by Simon Usher, with the following cast:

ABE, Tony Rohr

DARK WOMAN, Veronica Quilligan

PERAGRIN'S DAUGHTER, Susannah Doyle

Designer: Anthony Lamble

ABE comes into view. He is forty years old and wears an old double-breasted suit with a yellow flower in the lapel. His dirty dark hair is tucked behind his ears and reaches his collar. He has a slight limp.

He ambles along, is about to speak when PERAGRIN'S DAUGHTER arrives at his elbow. She is young and dirty and tired out.

ABE goes and stands next to the DARK WOMAN. She has flaming red hair with dark brown roots and wears pale shaded glasses. Her old nylon track suit top is greasy and so are her trousers. For the moment she wears a bridal veil atop her hair.

ABE: This land is full of fine women. Full of fine people
The love of a good woman. Keep the wolf from your door

'Step up O'Driscoll to the altar
Where'll we find a priest? Ask in the vestry.
At this time of the morning? He's fast asleep in his
    hammock.
What time is it? Six o'clock. Six o'clock in the morning.
Well tell him Dermot, the charmer of all England, is here
wanting to take the pledge and get married.
They won't let you. They won't let you
not with the smell of John Barleycorn on your teeth.'
'Alright then, I'll take my teeth out.'
Got a big laugh, that one

'Come on lads, jostle him up the aisle.
What a roaring party we've got here!
And who's that standing by the altar rail in a sunbeam?
In the slanted rays of the dawn sun?
Why, it's Mrs James.'

The love of a very good woman

'We've had some laughs with Mrs James haven't we lads?
Why does she call herself that? Wanted to impress.
She's in love with him. In love!'
Mrs James stood in a sunbeam, her flaming red hair,
roots like ashes.

I knew it was not to be.

'Quick lads, quick, stand them together. Light those candles!

At half past six they dragged the priest away from his sleeping pillow and pulled an antimacassock over his head and brought him screaming blue murder to the altar, his neck in a halter.

My bride. Oh my bride

*   *   *

PERAGRIN'S DAUGHTER joins ABE with a guitar.

ABE: OK

P.D.: Yeah, yeah. Hmmm

ABE: OK (*Puts his hand out for the guitar.*)

P.D.: Eh? Oh yeah (*Hands him a bottle.*)

ABE: No

P.D.: Oh. Oh yeah (*Hands him the guitar.*)

ABE: Unpack it then

P.D.: Ah! (*Sighs.*) Yeah. Yeah (*Nervously unpacks the guitar from its case.*)

ABE: Right (*Pause. He looks at her.*)

P.D.: Oh (*Moves back away behind a post.*)

ABE: What have you been doing to it?

P.D.: Oh

ABE: What?

P.D.: It's out of tune isn't it

ABE: Yeah it's out of tune

P.D.: Whew! Hey, do you want some?

ABE: What's the matter?

P.D.: Hot. It's hot

ABE: This is out of tune, you must have bumped it

P.D.: Ah. (*Sighs.*) Yeah, I bumped it I think. Whew! (*Drinks.*)

ABE: Ah. (*Sighs.*) Where's the bag?

P.D.: Here, here! (*Holds it out.*)

ABE: Yep. The bag has got to be here, with me for the coins to fall into

P.D.: Abe

ABE: Yes my dear?

P.D.: Play a song

ABE: I'm going to. I need a new string

P.D.: Mm (*Bites her lip, straightens her sleeve, sits down.*)

ABE: People

P.D.: Where? (*Getting up.*)

ABE: It looks bad, you've got to stand up. And away (*Waves her away.*)

P.D.: (*Worried.*) Oh Abe!

ABE: You'll be alright

P.D.: OK (*Straightens her sleeve, puts her hair behind her ear.*)

ABE: (*Finds a new string, tunes up.*)

P.D.: Abe, Abe

ABE: Mm?

P.D.: Can we go?

ABE: We only just arrived

P.D.: I know. I know we did. But. Yeah

Pause.

Abe, can we go now?

ABE: Ow! I broke my finger nail

P.D.: Abe

*   *   *

ABE joins the DARK WOMAN.

ABE: Outside the crowds of creditors gathered calling my
name and blowing their whistles in the cold morning
air. And inside the church, squatting behind statues,
their agents, bailiffs, mad dogs of women, anyone with
a grievance against me, all hiding there unnoticed in
the merry throng

Does a poor man deserve to marry in the clear sunlight
of a spring morning?
In a little city church with black walls and bedecked with
flowers?
They hired a piper to play, we even borrowed a ring for
the poor girls finger.
We shoved the man of God into his church and pressed
the word of God into his hand.
'Don't be paying any mind to that lot outside. It's just the
local residents complaining about the hullabaloo. The
traffic has come to a halt outside y'know, oh yes. There
are hordes of them out there. How do you know so many
people? They want your blood. We've just had word
from the police that they can't guarantee our protection.
Better crank that priest up a bit.

Come on your holyship, spit the words out!'

Thump, thump, thump! Bang, bang, bang!

ABE clutches onto the DARK WOMAN's arm in fright. She stares ahead hopefully.

Someone's a-thumping on the doors. Don't let them in Mary!

'Driscoll,' thundered the voice from outside. 'What about your little farm you left behind at home? The pigs lay dying, go home and feed them!'

Yes, and do you know why??! You businessmen have bought up my little farm and turned it into a slaughter-house. You developed me! And now I'm in debt

'Don't lie Driscoll, for we all know that you left your little farm and the little piggies without a word of goodbye, and went off to seek your fortune. We all know that Driscoll, ask your poor mam!'

Mammy, mammy

'Oh yes Driscoll. You went off to some fine place didn't you!'
Yes! And what did I find when I got there?
You! You lot were there waiting for me, dogging my every step.
You owned the very ground I walked on.

Don't heed them my love. We'll be married don't you fret

DARK WOMAN: I hear you don't have any collateral.
I suppose you haven't even the price of a bowl of soup

ABE: A bowl of soup my love? Are you hungry? If you can just hold on the bridal breakfast will be ready for you

'Look out Mrs James is putting him through his paces. Look at him jump! Oh well, isn't she a fine one, when you consider that the trousers she's got on her are dripping grease'

'Never you mind all that now Driscoll. The thing is you owe us some rent...'

Go to the devil for your rent!

He shakes his fist about him in all directions.

Bang! Bang! Thump!

More banging?

'Do you think they'll bust the doors down? Do you think they will?
Scandalous!'

'Driscoll. Driscoll?'

What is it?

'And where will you be living with your bride?'

Never mind that! Never mind that! Leave me alone!
We have a place don't you worry!

'Oh yes? And would that be a little house with a blue door and a few broken windows where we've seen you of late?'

I don't know what colour the door is!

'But Driscoll! You shouldn't be in that house! No, no, because it's not your own! You don't seriously think you can squat your little arse down on those floorboards do you?'

Why ever not? (*Weakly.*)

'You must know surely that we own that house Driscoll'

*   *   *

PERAGRIN'S DAUGHTER at his elbow on the left hand side.

P.D.: I need a toilet

ABE: You've already been this morning

P.D.: (*Shakes her head and whimpers a bit.*)

ABE: Go in the station

P.D.: Yeah. You come with me

ABE: No go on, you go, you'll be alright

P.D.: You go with me

ABE: What's the matter? Are you feeling nervous?

P.D.: (*Stares ahead, thinks, moves her hair, straightens her sleeve.*)
Yeah, yeah (*Nods.*)

ABE: Alright. Just go to the toilet. I'll wait here and then
we'll start, OK? Everything will be fine

P.D.: No, it's alright. I'll wait

ABE: OK

*   *   *

ABE: (*Seizes P.D.*) And with that the little devils rose up
from behind the statues of the Mother of God in the
middle of our ceremony and four and twenty mad
women danced towards me and seized me by the arms
and dragged me through the bewildered crowd of my
wedding guests, and raised me up onto their shoulders
like I was a coffin and did a jig out through the doors
bearing me aloft and delivered me up to my enemies.
It was all over

P.D.: Mind your guitar

ABE: But saddest of all, the last sight I saw, was out of
the corner of my eye as they carried me away; my
weeping bride, her red, red hair falling down into her
face, fainting into the arms of the blacksuited bailiffs,
the borrowed ring slipping from her finger

The DARK WOMAN drifts away.

P.D.: What's the matter?

ABE: I think I can see the back door. The future that used to be ahead is already in the past without ever having been in the present

P.D.: Would you like a drink from my bottle?

She feeds him it.

There, drink it back. That's it

ABE: How like my mother you sound. And you so young. Don't start mothering until your teats are properly developed or you'll have trouble later on

P.D.: Come home with me

ABE: You haven't a home

P.D.: I'd like to have one

ABE: That's where we are different. I have one but I can't go to it.

I've been on the road now many a year, hounded from lay-by to lay-by

I'd love to give up the roaming life. Perhaps go back and find the woman who...

I left her to fend for herself. I've heard she's wandering about in this vicinity herself these days.
I hope one day to run into her

I met an old boy the other day said she's quite well-to-do now. I don't know how he would know. Still, I trust she's been faithful. She hadn't much option with the eight kids I left on her lap

P.D.: (*Tucks her hair behind her ear and straightens her sleeve.*)

ABE: Yes, it's a fine thing. Of course ours are scattered to the four corners of the earth; residing in orphanages under false names

How will we ever get them back? It's all I live for but
they're hidden from us. They are brainwashing them
I expect, turning them against us. It's the old story.
I expect to be arrested by one of my sons one day

'Son,' I'll say, 'go on put the shackles on me.' And he'll
say, 'Daddy, why did you leave us alone in the trailer
undernourished and starving like you did?'

What good telling him I was walking up the road to
fetch water and a few bottles of milk when the social
worker stole them away. How could the little ones
understand that?

'You didn't love us, Daddy,' he'll say. 'If you had loved
us you wouldn't have let them take us away.'
What good saying I was tricked by the constables and
held by the arms in the police station?

P.D.: You can have new children with me

ABE: New children? I'm afraid... no, you're too young.
For all I know you could be my own

P.D.: Grandchildren then, have grandchildren with me

ABE: (*Suddenly lost.*) Where are we? Where are we going?

P.D.: You're with me. I'll look after you

ABE: You? Who are you? Can you spare a pound?

P.D.: Yes, yes, look (*She struggles a few coins from her pocket.*)

ABE: (*He stares at her dirty palm.*) God bless you, it's not
enough. Keep it. Save it up. Add to it. Then one day
you'll have a pound

P.D.: I'll help you find her

ABE: No, no, I know where she is

P.D.: I've already had many children. Growing. In here.
Do you see my hair?

ABE: Your hair, yes...

P.D.: It's different today –

ABE: Child –

P.D.: It could be. Look. (*She splays out her lank hair in her fingers.*) It is isn't it? It means there's another one growing inside

ABE: Let me go

P.D.: Are you going now?

ABE: Am I going now? Yes, yes. I'm going. Just help me rest a while first, then I'll go. Move those things so I can sit down

P.D.: There isn't anything

ABE: Isn't there? I thought there was something

P.D.: (*Prepares for him to sit down. He doesn't. She tucks her hair behind her ear, she straightens her sleeve.*) I feel like a lioness

ABE: When you are both very tired, an extra companion can join you, or sometimes just a piece of luggage. It's an hallucination

*   *   *

The DARK WOMAN wheels up and down on her balcony. ABE is in the street below.

ABE: 'Open this door! (*He thumps the door, he laughs.*) Open up!'

DARK WOMAN: (*Lifts herself out of her wheelchair and hangs over the balcony then slumps back into her chair.*) Oh it's you

ABE: 'It's the bailiffs, come to get you out'

DARK WOMAN: 'Oh yes, well, I'm occupied in drawing up my husband's accounts Your Lordship'

ABE: 'I shall be wanting to look at those infamous documents too!'

DARK WOMAN: 'They're nearly finished but not quite'

ABE: 'Then madam I must conclude that you can barely be numerate'

DARK WOMAN: Don't start flaunting your airs and graces!

ABE: 'Come on out of there you old biddy!'

DARK WOMAN: Don't push your luck (*She throws a bottle at him.*) Clear off!

ABE: You don't want to end up an old soak on the streets but then, who does? And then, why shouldn't it be you? I don't see you inviting the homeless in off the streets

DARK WOMAN: (*Trying to lift herself up in agitation.*) Liar! Just give me the power to walk and you'll never see me again. You can keep the rotten stinking house, I don't want it!

ABE: But you can walk surely?

DARK WOMAN: (*In tears, angry.*) I can't, I can't!

ABE: Oh come on now, a little bit surely...

DARK WOMAN: I can't. Why don't you look at this – (*She cries, thumping her wheelchair.*)

Pause.

ABE: 'Ah, now we're not hard men. Tell us, you must have had a little accident, no?'

DARK WOMAN: 'I did Sir, yes. An accident with the stairs. Long ago. And I'm still a cripple from it'

ABE: 'Oh is that so? Yes, that's bad'

DARK WOMAN: (*Cries.*) Yes, I can't bloody walk!

ABE: 'It's a pity because we want the house. It's your husband you see. Never paid a debt since the day you married him. Could you tell me why that is?'

DARK WOMAN: 'Well the truth of it is Your Lordship, he has no money'

ABE: 'Ah, no money, no money, poor man. Well, if you could see your way to helping us out with a few bob on his behalf it will go favourably for him when we next consider his case'

DARK WOMAN: Consider his case all you want, it's nothing to do with me

ABE: But a few pence to keep body and soul together...

DARK WOMAN: I have nothing!

ABE: Alright then, I'll leave you here in your shame!

DARK WOMAN: There's no shame here except the shame of he who left me

ABE: I wish I could believe that

DARK WOMAN: (*Starts coughing.*)

ABE: What's the matter?

DARK WOMAN: Nothing (*Coughs more.*)

ABE: You should rest. Stay inside in the warm

DARK WOMAN: Shut up. I don't want to

She coughs herself into exhaustion.

*   *   *

ABE turns to PERAGRIN'S DAUGHTER who turns away.

ABE: Well my child, what can I do for you?

You do recognise me I hope?

I am a married man as you can see

Hand me my stick can you boy. Thankee

I have suffered a few little bits of damage to my leg on account of things not being properly screwed down on deck

Whoops! (*He reels and regains his balance as if they are on a ship.*)

What have we here? A cabin boy? Your hair is exceeding long. Come with me boy...

P.D.: (*Tucks her hair behind her ear and straightens her sleeve.*)

ABE: Don't worry (*He takes a few steps away and rolls a cigarette.*)

They stand staring in opposite directions unable to talk. PERAGRIN'S DAUGHTER steals a glance at his back then he turns and looks over his shoulder.

Hello there

P.D.: (*Looks away.*)

ABE turns to her holding his cigarette.

ABE: If you ask me I'd say you don't look very well

P.D.: (*Looks at him, straightens her sleeve, tucks her hair behind her ear and turns away.*)

ABE: Got a light?

P.D.: (*Searches her pockets.*)

ABE: (*Goes to her.*) The ship I was on, the Captain had smuggled his wife on board dressed as a cabin boy. This was bringing the ship bad luck, and in the middle of a great tempest we forced him to confess his deception. We made him tie her up and throw her overboard, to save all our lives. Poor man how he wept lamenting his selfishness. (*He takes PERAGRIN'S DAUGHTER by the shoulders and indicates the sea with his arm.*) And in the very moment that the girl's white dresses were bobbing around in the waves the waters became calm again

P.D. : (*Straightens her sleeve.*)

ABE: Yes, calm waters

P.D.: (*Strikes him a match.*)

ABE: Thankee

> Aren't you a little bit young to be out on the streets on your own?

A dog barks in a back yard far away.

> The debt she has is all my own

The dog barks some more.

> But as you can see, she has reached levels of hypocrisy and chicanery that leaves the likes of me, a simple working man, a peasant by birth, leaves me standing.

P.D.: Let's go, Abe

ABE: It's a wild life isn't it? People here, people there. Who can tell? Who knows what's going on eh? Who knows?

> I've been around

P.D.: Abe –

ABE: (*To himself about P.D.*) Funny thing is, when you get up close she's got a peculiar smell

P.D.: ?

ABE: Like a fox's arse. An attractive person all in all, but aromatic, in an odd way

> We shall play truant together. You play truant, I'll collect the social security

> Thank goodness I'm here to help you

P.D.: Yes

ABE: Where's your daddy?

P.D.: Daddy...

ABE: He should be here to protect you, shouldn't he?
Should I take you to the sea? Can you drive? No?
A pity, we could have gone on holiday together

P.D.: I don't want to go on holiday with you –

ABE: Why not?

P.D.: (*In a sudden outburst.*) You keep writing all your letters to
me telling me what great friends we are but you could be
mistaken – That's why!

ABE: (*Taken aback.*) But I've never written a letter to you in
my life. Why, I hardly know you

P.D.: (*Holding her hands in front of her face.*) Sorry! The letters
you leave for her

ABE: You've been reading my letters?

P.D.: You never seal them

ABE: No, I never seal them. It thrills me to think that others
might read them

P.D.: They're beautiful letters...

ABE: I'm just glad somebody reads them. They are
composed by the engine-room mechanic. He's a
romantic genius. Talking of genius. Have I shown
you this?

He produces a newspaper cutting from his pocket and hands it to her.

It's a friend of mine actually. Seems to be doing rather
well doesn't he. We were at school together. Great pals

P.D.: (*Checking both sides.*) It's an advertisement

ABE: What? Here. Let me see (*He snatches it.*) I've cut out the
wrong bit!

*   *   *

Night-time. ABE leads PERAGRIN'S DAUGHTER.

ABE: Look, it's early evening. There's no moon. It's very dark. That's just how I like it

You see this line of trees?

P.D.: No

ABE: Let's just say there's a line of trees. Strange trees, short, knotted, like dwarfed trees

P.D.: Yes

ABE: I must say, it rather spoils the effect that you can't see them. Surely your young eyes...?

P.D.: (*Looks vaguely.*)

ABE: Alright

P.D.: Listen, can you help me?

ABE: Well

P.D.: I need a drink

ABE: It's easy. Just hold your breath, tip your head back...

PERAGRIN'S DAUGHTER faints, he catches her.

You shouldn't roll your eyes too far back into your head

She comes to.

Look on the bright side, this can't go on forever

P.D.: Take me home

ABE: I can't. Whoops! (*He reels again then balances as if they are on a ship.*) Look at that. We've hit a storm

P.D.: (*Produces a bottle.*) Rum?

ABE: Certainly

P.D.: I have to go to the toilet

ABE: You go too often, it makes you thin. Try to slow down
your metabolism

P.D.: My doctor says I have a fast heartbeat. Feel

ABE: I'm not a doctor. I wouldn't know where to look

P.D.: Here (*She puts his hand to the jugular vein in her neck.*)

ABE: (*Immediately.*) Very fast. Perhaps you should sit down

P.D.: And here (*Under her breast.*)

ABE: ... my life is... I'd like to explain

P.D.: I'd like to go to the toilet

ABE: I went to her father. Father-in-law, I said, lend me a
thousand pounds. I can't, he said, I have responsibilities
to my race, we are a wandering tribe. I gave him ten
pounds of my own and said, 'Take this and wander away
as far as you like.' She's from a persecuted people

A lorry goes past, it has a whining wheel that screams loudly, fades.

P.D.: (*Takes a few steps.*) I like cities

ABE: So do I

P.D.: They make me feel so warm inside

ABE: Where are you going?

P.D.: So warm inside

ABE: And of course that business with the pigs. Men in
suits kept coming around and bothering her when
I wasn't there to protect her. They tried to shift all
the blame for that onto her shoulders. They sent her
photographs, horrible, horrible things, with demands
for payment. I don't deny it made her life a misery

P.D.: I'm feeling the inside of my cage

ABE: And what with the children running about all over the place from God knows where, booted around from corner to corner

P.D.: I'm like a wounded animal in the zoo

ABE: I must go

P.D.: Let me come with you

ABE: With me? I would but I'm not really going anywhere.

Pause.

Let me give you a little advice

P.D.: Not now

ABE: Why not?

P.D.: I'm haemorrhaging

ABE: The advice is this...

P.D.: (*Cries in pain.*)

ABE: If you ever let something take root in you...

P.D.: Am I having a baby?

ABE: ... it'll be like one of those trees

P.D.: Oh! (*In pain.*)

ABE: Strange old pixies of trees aren't they?

P.D.: Please...

ABE: Oh God!

He holds her fainting in his arms.

How long will this go on for?

P.D.: This is your fault

ABE: (*Holds her.*) My poor child. Don't worry. I was attracted by your negative qualities. You, you fill up the dark side of a man. You are the invisible side of my soul

P.D.: Do you love me?

ABE: Love?

P.D.: All men love me

ABE: You're mistaken...

P.D.: Abe

ABE: Ester, Ester, help me

P.D.: Who's that you're calling?

ABE: My wife. She did first aid I remember

PERAGRIN'S DAUGHTER collapses.

Get up, get up, I'm not finished. Gentle soul
She deserves better than this.

I thought somehow I could encourage you with my positive qualities you see and that between us a more or less equal librium would be established until we got you to a toilet or even something better, who knows.

But now. Oh get up please!

P.D.: (*Muttering.*) All men love me

ABE: Hush, hush, who needs to know that?

*   *   *

ABE wheels the DARK WOMAN in her wheelchair, they come through the door and along the balcony. ABE wheels slowly. The DARK WOMAN has sunglasses on. The bright morning sun shines onto her face. She squints into it, brushing the hair back off her cheeks.

ABE: Coffee?

DARK WOMAN: Mm

ABE: Doughnuts?

DARK WOMAN: Mm yes!

ABE goes in.

A lorry goes by with a whining wheel.

Sounds of children playing come drifting from a school playground.

The DARK WOMAN leans on the balcony sunning her face, listening and watching.

ABE reappears. Two coffees, doughnuts in a paper bag.

DARK WOMAN: Where did you get them?

ABE: I nipped out earlier while you were still asleep

DARK WOMAN: Then you came back and scared me

ABE: You thought I was the police

DARK WOMAN: Yes I did

ABE: Doughnuts?

DARK WOMAN: Thanks

ABE: Coffee

DARK WOMAN: Isn't it a wonderful morning

ABE: Yes, yes it is

DARK WOMAN: It is, Abe

Pause.

It's nice of you to wheel me around a bit this morning, my fingers ache so much... Abe?

ABE: Yes?

DARK WOMAN: There is a thing you could do for me. I'd love it...

ABE: What?

DARK WOMAN: Lift me out of this chair

ABE: Lift you?

DARK WOMAN: Pick me up. Take me in your arms as if I were your little daughter or something and hold me up so I can see over the balcony rail. Would you do that?

ABE: I'll do that...

DARK WOMAN: (*Stares at him and smiles.*) I'll just put down my coffee cup. There. Alright. I'm ready

ABE lifts her out of her wheelchair.

They stare at each other.

ABE: Aren't you going to look then?

DARK WOMAN: Look? Oh yes, yes (*She doesn't look.*) Put me down please Abe

ABE: Down?

DARK WOMAN: Yes please

ABE: (*He sets her down in the wheelchair again. Pause.*) Well, what did you see?

DARK WOMAN: (*Holding her head in her hands.*) Nothing

ABE: You want to get out and about a bit

DARK WOMAN: You say that! I never wanted to live here. You brought me here against my will

ABE: I did not

DARK WOMAN: Against my will!

ABE: This was our home

DARK WOMAN: Not to me it wasn't

ABE: Not to you

DARK WOMAN: Don't try to be surprised

ABE: I'm not surprised

DARK WOMAN: You shouldn't be! Locking me in here!

ABE: I'm sorry... I wasn't able to be here with you... more often

DARK WOMAN: You never lived here!

ABE: No, sadly

DARK WOMAN: Oh yes, the great man, free to roam

ABE: Exiled

DARK WOMAN: Oh your fine words! Your fine words! And all your friends and all your women –

ABE: I have no friends. And all the women I have kissed goodbye long ago

DARK WOMAN: While I rot!

ABE: I promise you I am as lonely as you

DARK WOMAN: Rot in this ditch

ABE: It was to be our marital ditch

DARK WOMAN: I never wanted it. You'd have me a little bird on your window sill

ABE: A little bird?

DARK WOMAN: These are walls of a prison to me. This is not the way of my people. I want the whisper of the moon, the trickle of the old faucet...

ABE: Well, you've been here so long now so why not stop complaining? If I could I'd help you. I'd do anything.

But what can I do? You're in that chair and well, we're stuck with it

DARK WOMAN: (*With venom.*) Don't mention the chair

ABE: I should mention it

DARK WOMAN: Oh you love it don't you!

ABE: It's our problem isn't it...

DARK WOMAN: Oh yes!

ABE: And because of it you can't ever leave the house. It's true, I have to say it

DARK WOMAN: Don't... just don't

ABE: Don't what woman?

DARK WOMAN: Don't...

ABE: You are bitter. You are. Bitter. I don't blame you. I'd be bitter

DARK WOMAN: ... dare

ABE: It's the drink talking now

DARK WOMAN: You–!

ABE: Isn't it?

DARK WOMAN: Oh yes, the fine man! Tell me. Tell me more, what shall I do daddio. What would you advise that I do? Do you have any great ideas?

ABE: It was you, drunk, fell down the stairs

DARK WOMAN: Oh yes!

ABE: Down the stairs and broke your back

DARK WOMAN: Oh was it? Was it really?

ABE: Oh God, can you see it now? The little children standing outside for the ambulance. Oh our Mammy has broken her neck and she's going to be dead. Oh our Mammy nearly killed our poor dad as well with a kitchen knife when he tried to stop her.

DARK WOMAN: (*Starts up a scream.*)

ABE: Oh our Mammy is screaming now as she screamed then. Isn't she? Doesn't she scream with the best of them? And didn't we once hear her say Daddy doesn't touch her no more. And is that a dirty thing? Because Daddy seemed ashamed

DARK WOMAN: (*A high pitched wail.*) Go away!

ABE: Then you drove the little kiddies away. And now they'll never come back

DARK WOMAN: I did not drive them away!

ABE: As soon as my back was turned. I'd only just popped out. Cast them out!

DARK WOMAN: No, no Abe

ABE: I was only just fetching a loaf of bread and some matches!

DARK WOMAN: Oh you're so cruel!

ABE: The little darlings, we haven't seen them since. It backfired on you didn't it, your dirty trick? You couldn't get them back could you?

DARK WOMAN: It was the police took them, and that woman with glasses, they threw them in the van

ABE: That was your revenge wasn't it?

DARK WOMAN: No, no they was screaming to me, 'Mam! Mam!' They knew I wanted them to stay. The police held me back, they pushed me on the floor.

ABE: You fell over, you were too drunk

DARK WOMAN: It was in the morning, I hadn't had a drink. I was, I was looking for their breakfast

ABE: There wasn't any breakfast

DARK WOMAN: I was looking...

ABE: There was nothing except margarine

DARK WOMAN: Yes and why was that? You'd not bought any food, not even for your own children could you produce even a bit of bread and milk

ABE: How could I? There was no money

DARK WOMAN: No money! Why didn't you earn some money

ABE: I tried!

DARK WOMAN: Oh yes, you tried. You couldn't even feed your own children

ABE: They wouldn't let me on the gangs

DARK WOMAN: They could see what kind you were

ABE: They wouldn't let me...

DARK WOMAN: Good enough for you!

ABE: You wicked woman!

DARK WOMAN: Oh yes I'm wicked. Didn't you know? I'm evil actually. Watch out I don't put a spell on you

ABE: You've already done that. My whole life, my children

DARK WOMAN: I put a spell on my own children? I'll kill you if you don't get out

ABE: Kill me, I don't care. It will be a relief to all of us

DARK WOMAN: And listen to the self-pity now. Listen to the self-pity of the man who couldn't keep his children from the law

Pause.

*   *   *

A roadside. A line of washing strung from one tree to another. Rain is falling.

ABE: It was very dull to live in a country where there is nothing. You're never ahead. Always behind

Pause.

Poverty is a terrible thing.

That's what I like about this place. Everyone is so rich. It's wonderful

Pause.

I suppose my washing is wet from the rain

P.D.: Yeah, it got wet

ABE: Never mind. We'll have to get a lift in to a launderette. In town. We'll get a lift in a lorry (*Stands up.*)

I like the countryside. It makes you feel so warm. Inside

P.D.: Where are we going?

ABE: I'm just glad to get some fresh air. I belong to the wind, I'm at home in the mud and the fields, when the trees are dripping water, I'm at home. On the day I left, didn't a little chicken come up to me in the dust and kneel down begging me to stay?

P.D.: I'm not afraid of being on my own

ABE: You're very lucky

P.D.: I've been like it since the day I was born

ABE: It's strange how lucky some people are

P.D.: (*Suddenly looks at him.*) We've been through so much together

ABE: Have we? Wait. There's a strange sweetness in the air. What is this taste in my mouth?

P.D.: (*Gets up.*)

ABE: Where are you going?

A lorry approaches with a whining wheel.

P.D.: I'll get a lift on my own

ABE: I'll come with you

P.D.: It'll be quicker with just one

ABE: I dare say

P.D.: Bye

PERAGRIN'S DAUGHTER goes.

ABE: (*Quietly, not calling.*) Come back. Strange girl

Pause.

(*Calls out.*) My washing! I suppose I'll have to take it down myself. Haven't I given you my all?

Gets up. Shivers.

Embers of the fire, what shall I do now? The girl has left me.

What a long decade it has been.

I need a job. I need a wife. I need a home!

I'd better get cracking or this could go on for ever.

He takes down his drying suit and wrings out the rainwater. He drops the clothes into the mud.

Where's my tin whistle?

Where is my comb?

Where is my framed photograph?

(*He picks up his clothes.*) My clothes are covered in mud.

(*Hugs them to him.*) The whole roadside is awash with mud.
It's a sea of mud. Ship ahoy! (*He sticks his thumb up to a lorry
passing a long way off.*)

Didn't I give you my all?

He dresses in his wet muddy suit and shirt.

(*Calls out.*) Don't you think I need the things you need?

My all was not a lot to give.

My all was not a lot to give.

It's cold. Is there anyone out there? I have the falling
sickness (*Falls.*) My eyes. Can't anyone come forward?
I'm growing weak. The sugar in my blood, it isn't
enough! A Mars Bar; someone please help (*He struggles
in the mud, holding his head.*) Mamma, Mamma

PERAGRIN'S DAUGHTER comes back.

P.D.: Look what I found

ABE: (*From the mud.*) Mud...

P.D.: A suitcase

ABE: Muddy, mud...

P.D.: It's empty

ABE: I'm not a well man

P.D.: What is it?

ABE: Well, my father died of sclerosis of the liver

P.D.: Oh

ABE: I can't remember if it's hereditary

P.D.: (*Straightens her sleeve.*)

ABE: I'm sorry you should find me like this

P.D.: (*Tucks her hair behind her ear.*)

ABE: (*Still groping in the mud.*) You can see what a wild rover I would have been if it wasn't for this infirmity I have. Muddy, mud...

P.D.: Listen shall I help you up or something?

ABE: You're hardly up to it

P.D.: Here (*Puts out her arm.*)

ABE: Can we not head off this awful moment in some other way. Let me turn on my back so I can see you. We can talk

P.D.: I have to go

ABE: You've only just arrived

P.D.: My mother will be wondering where I am

ABE: I remember the name

P.D.: My mother

ABE: Your mother?

P.D.: My mother will be wondering where I am

ABE: Yes, I remember. Well, thanks for all your help in washing my clothes. Unfortunately they're dirty again. You should have seen me on my wedding day

A lorry with a whining wheel travels past.

A lorry. It's wheel was whining.

What a marvelous landscape

P.D.: I think we'll be friends for ever

ABE: You say the nicest things

P.D.: I like you very much and I hope you will always be
my friend

ABE: Yes surely. I'll write you a letter. Oh no, I forgot,
you've already been getting my letters to my wife.
I know, you just keep on reading those. I'll hold you
in mind while I write them in future

P.D.: I think one day we'll, we'll be a great pair together
and people will talk about us in the same breath always...

ABE: What a wonderful future you have planned for us.
I only hope we run into each other sometimes so it can
all come true

P.D.: Bye (*Goes.*)

ABE: Yes goodbye (*Lies back in the mud.*)

How can I forget that smell.

I wonder will she come back again? We could take the
road together. She promised eternal friendship.

What a wonderful thing. I've got to get moving.

Hunger and Cold. Hunger and Cold.

*   *   *

*ABE and the DARK WOMAN roll out onto the balcony together.
She has her bridal veil on her head.*

DARK WOMAN: What are you doing here anyway?

ABE: I found myself here

DARK WOMAN: (*Inaudibly.*) Get out of my house

ABE: This! This spot is the meeting place of everyone
thrown out of here! Here give me your hand. Who

brought you here? Those years ago. Recount for
me now

DARK WOMAN: I fought my way in by myself you fool.
    For all the help you were I might as well have stayed
    put. They didn't want women of my race here for fear
    we'd light fires. But I showed them.

ABE: Ah, you swept me off my feet

DARK WOMAN: And from that very day they haven't
    left me a moment's peace. Why didn't you keep them
    from me?

ABE: If you must know, I followed my little babbies around
    from a distance where they couldn't see me. And in this
    four-cornered world I tried to keep them from harm

DARK WOMAN: Oh, is that it?

ABE: It is my true story

DARK WOMAN: Oh, and I'll tell you mine. With the first
    baby born they came and pulled the blankets from the
    windows and pulled off the door, with the second came
    the summons for arrears of rent, with the third they came
    and put barbed wire around our garden, with little Kerry
    number four they said they'd burn me if there were any
    more, with number five they took away the steel and
    iron you'd left rotting here – You'd better get out lassie
    and take your brood with you, God rot them! – and with
    number six they chased me away and before number
    seven they had chased me back again and wouldn't let
    me go

    And if you were looking for them how come you never
    found them?

ABE: Never found them? Oh but the roads were long, very,
    very long. I'd no idea where even to start.

DARK WOMAN: You've no cunning. I come from a line
of cunning men. You fell for their tricks all along, didn't
you?

ABE: I did, I did. They told me – If yous can get a house
fit to live in you can have your kiddies back. But when
I went to ask for a house do you know what they said?
If you can get your kiddies back you can have a house
Oh, if they'd rolled the Earth as flat as they've rolled
you and me, we'd have fallen off the edge of it long ago

DARK WOMAN: Go away from me now. You stink the
stink of loneliness. You're desperate about every minute
and every night, aren't you! Well, I'm not. I think of it
year by year, and I've never fallen to my knees in the
small hours in front of the mirror and asked – who, who,
who will speak to me? –

ABE: (*Looking over the balcony rail at the world.*) Yes, I know,
I hate to leave you though. Can you manage in the dark
with the wheelchair and the stairs, isn't it very difficult?
I would stay and help you

DARK WOMAN: What? And have them catch you here in
the morning?

ABE: Well, if you do see one of the babbies, take him in

DARK WOMAN: You don't need to tell me that. And if
you see one?

ABE: If it's a boy give him a kick, if it's a girl give her a
milk stout

He smiles at her, she laughs.

*   *   *

ABE is at the roadside, PERAGRIN'S DAUGHTER comes back.

ABE: Are you still here?

Haven't you got a home to go to?

P.D.: Of course I have

ABE: You could introduce me to all your friends

P.D.: They've all gone

ABE: I expect they are busy with their jobs

P.D.: Yes

ABE: (*Pause.*) Maybe they will want to help us?

P.D.: Who?

ABE: Help me up then and we'll carry on by ourselves.
Guided by our own pure thoughts we'll think of one
thing and one thing only

P.D.: What?

ABE: It doesn't matter, God will inform us

She helps him up.

We'll earn money. We'll meet lots of people.
We'll get everyone, bring them all with us

P.D.: Don't you want me for yourself?

ABE: Ah this time of day! It's a Sunday, hot and dusty,
the empty motorway stretches out ahead of us in the
heat. So peaceful. That way lies America, the great
unknown continent, and that way sober Asia with her
undiscovered vale of tears. To the south, Africa, my
brothers and sisters grinding two solitary grains on a
stone, their caravans are coming this way...

P.D.: Don't you want me for yourself?

ABE: Oh if only you didn't need money to travel I would
be a nomad myself

P.D.: I don't feel well

ABE: No, you feel alright don't you?

P.D.: I'm ill

ABE: What do you need?

P.D.: (*Moans gently.*)

ABE: I know a man. If we go to him tomorrow he can get you access to a hospital bed

P.D.: No (*Moans.*)

ABE: Is there nothing I can give you? I know, we can walk to the sea. Eastbourne. You'd love it. I know a couple of nurses there, they said I was very avant-garde (*He laughs fondly.*)

P.D.: Oh! (*She groans.*)

ABE: Where's your ma?

P.D.: She remarried

ABE: Oh my poor darling!

P.D.: Are you falling in love with me?

ABE: It's difficult to love the sick –

P.D.: Aren't you

ABE: – except to learn to minister the suffering Christ in them

P.D.: (*Holding her stomach.*) Can't you love me?

ABE: Can you be the suffering Christ?

P.D.: I'm not well enough

Falls to her knees and would be sick but she lacks the strength.

ABE: Ah well, it's a long road, We'd better get started

P.D.: (*Feverish, weak, on the ground.*) No, no

ABE: And when night comes the dogs will bark, the shutters come down, and you and I, ... and everything will – ... you and I, we – ... you – ...

He looks down at her.

Are you ill? Shall I help you?

P.D.: Help me!

ABE: When I think of all the friends I've known who have gone down in this way. I remember even on my wedding day, my companions fell into the gutter like ashes into a pool...

It has become dusk, the sky is clear and darkening, a pale tint at its edge.

Do you need water? We haven't any

He takes off his coat.

P.D.: I need water!

ABE: Here, have my coat (*He lays it over her.*)

A dog barks.

Night falls.

*   *   *

ABE is standing below the balcony.

ABE: Madam! Madam! I know you're in there! I want a word! Stop your hiding!

PERAGRIN'S DAUGHTER appears on the balcony, her hair flowing and shining, well brushed; her lips like cherries, her eyes sparkling; but any look of health has finally disappeared.

P.D.: What do you want?

ABE: Please be so good as to get me your mistress

P.D.: My what?

ABE: Your employer

P.D.: My what?

ABE: Your mother, get her down here

P.D.: My what?

ABE: Your friend

P.D.: Listen

ABE: I look like this because of the way I live. It's a very traditional culture

P.D.: Listen, fuck it

ABE: It's a tradition of suffering and persecution. It's becoming very fashionable now you'll find

P.D.: Please don't

ABE: Look at my jewellery. My rings. Hand made. Stolen

PERAGRIN'S DAUGHTER goes in.

Come on

ABE takes out some mud from his jacket pocket and throws it at the window.

PERAGRIN'S DAUGHTER reappears.

ABE: Hello there. I wonder if I could have a word?

P.D.: Go on then

ABE: It's like this; I'm a born loser otherwise I'd ask you to come down and sort it out with blows

P.D.: Is that it?

ABE: You must be very busy

P.D.: Yes...

ABE: The only thing is, the rent is going up

P.D.: What?

ABE: The rent. Up. It goes as from today

P.D.: So what?

ABE: Also–

P.D.: So what? Because she doesn't pay it anyway

ABE: One more thing. We're repossessing the property

P.D.: What?

ABE: And then selling it

P.D.: So what's the point of putting the rent up?

ABE: We want to cover all the exits

P.D.: The what?

ABE: Exits. The exits. Cover all the exits. We want to –

P.D.: Yeah

ABE: So

P.D.: So what?

ABE: So if you'd tell her I'd like a word

The DARK WOMAN wheels onto the balcony.

DARK WOMAN: What is it honey?

P.D.: Nothing, it's nothing

ABE: It's me. (*Pause.*) I had an errand but I've forgotten it now

DARK WOMAN: Oh. Well, what are you trying to do?

ABE: I came –

DARK WOMAN: What's the point? Can't you see I can manage by myself

ABE: Yes, it's true

DARK WOMAN: I brought up your children, you never helped

ABE: I was on the high seas

DARK WOMAN: No you weren't

ABE: If the social security had paid up I might have settled down

DARK WOMAN: My life counted for nothing. My whole life you wasted

ABE: Just now, I was occupied momentarily. A young girl, barely literate but a great wit, tried to seduce me by spilling her bodily fluids on me. I resisted but she eclipsed my whole personality with her darkness.

Come away with me now and we'll lead a gay old life. I thought we could live on the land. I have a piece in mind. I brought some of it here in my pocket, look

DARK WOMAN: Leave me be

ABE: But what is left in store? Your children are gone. You have no home, no money, your health is failing. Bleak years ahead

DARK WOMAN: You want my house for yourself! That's it isn't it!

ABE: No, no. What would I gain from your moving away? You're the only person I know on this earth

DARK WOMAN: You'd enjoy the thrill of being totally alone

ABE: No, no woman!

PERAGRIN'S DAUGHTER appears below with her suitcase.

Another thing is, I think I may be going blind. I need someone to lead me about

DARK WOMAN: That is a very selfish thing

ABE: As you well know invalids must be iron-willed. You and I could go forth together up the A1. You have kith and kin residing on its banks. We can go and find them, they'll give us succour I know

P.D.: Go with him, I don't care

DARK WOMAN: I'll not go with him, you go with him

P.D.: I'm not going with him

DARK WOMAN: I'm not leaving this house

P.D.: I don't want your house if that's what you're thinking

ABE: Go inside child

P.D.: I'm not going inside, you go inside

ABE: I'm a little too old to go acting on advice

P.D.: (*To DARK WOMAN.*) Why don't you take what you're given. What's wrong with unhappiness. People should be unhappy. It's good for them

ABE: Your constant blessing, day in, day out, it's like a curse –

P.D.: Especially children. Look at me, I don't regret anything. When I was a child –

ABE: She's still only a child

P.D.: I had to lay in wait like a fox for my dinner...

ABE: (*To DARK WOMAN.*) I... I... Have no stronger argument

P.D.: (*She sways.*) But at least I'm alive... I'm glad –

ABE: (*Spits.*) God forgive me my ignorance

DARK WOMAN: God damn your ignorance!

ABE: Look, some children in pushchairs being trundled past. God, isn't that a sight!

Hello Mickey Mouse! Hello! Hello!

DARK WOMAN: Get away from me, leave us

P.D.: No, don't say that to him!

ABE: She's right. What's done is done and the future's never far behind

P.D.: (*Picks up her suitcase.*) Help me with this

ABE: (*Picks up the suitcase.*) This doesn't weigh a thing

P.D.: Just carry it a little way for me, that's it. Here, here come on

DARK WOMAN: You and your tricks

P.D.: I have a right!

DARK WOMAN: You have no right, you're just a child, leave him alone

P.D.: Just carry it to the corner for me and I'll wait for the bus

DARK WOMAN: Oh a bus now is it? Why don't you hop in a taxi? She's a little grand now isn't she!

P.D.: I am grand! I'm going to be grand. I'm alive, and... all my grandness and... my body... my whole body... People will kiss me

ABE: God bless the little one! You see Mary, you should learn that –

DARK WOMAN: Wake up now Dermot

ABE: I am awake. Are you in pain?

DARK WOMAN: Only my eyes

ABE: Who are you weeping for?

        *   *   *

PERAGRIN'S DAUGHTER appears on the balcony, her hair flowing and shining, well brushed; her lips like cherries, her eyes sparkling; but any look of health has finally disappeared.

ABE: I look like this because of the way I live. It's a very traditional culture

P.D.: Listen –

ABE: It's a tradition of suffering and persecution. It's becoming very fashionable now you'll find. It's like this; I'm a born loser otherwise –

P.D.: Is that it?

ABE: I'd like a word

P.D.: We're very busy

ABE: I know you are, Many have tried to steal her. I've let them. I stood by. Where is my stolen wife? Poor woman!

P.D.: Your wife?

ABE: My wife. My friend. My mistress

P.D.: She won't come out. Because they're repossessing the property. She's hiding

ABE: So what? (*He staggers towards the doorway and thumps on the door.*) Please, please! Mrs James! (*He is tearful.*) There's a man here to see you!

    Mrs James!

The DARK WOMAN comes onto the balcony.

DARK WOMAN: (*To P.D.*) What is it honey?

P.D.: He's come about the rent

ABE: She has the proper air of the business woman doesn't she?

DARK WOMAN: Leave her alone

ABE: She was the lonely child of the roadway when I knew her

P.D.: (*To ABE.*) Look what I've got here

ABE: What is it but an empty suitcase?

PERAGRIN'S DAUGHTER goes in.

ABE: Another thing is, I think I may be going blind.
I need someone to lead me about.

DARK WOMAN: That's a very selfish thing

ABE: Well as you know, invalids must be iron-willed. The alternative is oblivion.

PERAGRIN'S DAUGHTER comes back out.

P.D.: No, you're wrong, it's something else!

ABE: You and I could go forth together up the Al. You have kith and kin residing on its banks. We can go and find them, they'll give us succour I know

DARK WOMAN: I've had enough of your blab

PERAGRIN'S DAUGHTER comes forward.

P.D.: Abe, look inside

ABE: No, wait a minute –

P.D.: I lost the ugly duckling!

ABE: Isn't that what you wanted to happen?

P.D.: Yes but... Oh Abe! Hey do you want to see it?

ABE: What? (*He looks up for the DARK WOMAN but she is not there.*)

P.D.: I've got it here, I put it in this suitcase

ABE: You did?

P.D.: Yes I brought it here to you

ABE: To me? But Lord, I don't want it!

P.D.: (*In tears.*) No, no but –

> *She pulls back her tears, puts her hair behind hers ears and straightens her sleeve.*

> No, no wait until you see it. It's really nice. Sweet little thing

ABE: Stop it. Keep it away from me!

P.D.: (*Opens suitcase.*) Wait till you see it...

ABE: I don't want to see it!

P.D.: Why not?

ABE: It's a terrible thing to –

P.D.: But it's part of me!

ABE: It's not a part of you!

P.D.: But who is it a part of then?

ABE: No one! It's not a part of anyone!

P.D.: But it was growing in my body!

ABE: Listen...

P.D.: It's me!

ABE: No!

P.D.: Here you see (*Thoroughly defeated she nevertheless tries to present the suitcase to him.*)

ABE: No! (*Awkwardly he boots the suitcase away.*)

The DARK WOMAN appears at the doorway, standing.

PERAGRIN'S DAUGHTER picks up the dropped suitcase, she peeps at what's inside restoring the disturbed contents with her hand.

P.D.: No, I – (*She stumbles with the suitcase.*)

ABE: I'm sorry child

P.D.: (*Smiles awkwardly.*)

DARK WOMAN: Wake up now Dermot

ABE: I am awake

DARK WOMAN: Are you in pain?

ABE: Only my eyes

DARK WOMAN: Poor Abe!

ABE: Don't weep for me, weep for yourselves

P.D.: Would he like to rest his head on my suitcase?

ABE: Possibly

PERAGRIN'S DAUGHTER shoves the suitcase under his head.

The End.

A MESSAGE
FOR THE BROKEN HEARTED

Characters

MICKEY

LINDA

JENINE

MR. STEVENSON

A MESSAGE FOR THE BROKEN HEARTED was first performed at the Liverpool Playhouse Studio in March 1993. It was directed by Ramin Gray, with the following cast:

MICKEY, Kevin McMonagle

LINDA, Rose Keegan

JENINE, Samantha Holland

MR. STEVENSON, Maurice Perry

Designer: Nigel Prabavalkhar

PART ONE

Sitting on a bench in a garden.

LINDA: Mickey... do you think there's anything wrong with our relationship?

MICKEY: (*Smiles ironically.*)

LINDA: What's wrong do you think?

MICKEY: Out of chaos came disaster, then out of disaster came chaos, then out of chaos came disaster

LINDA: Oh. Don't you think it's because you're having an affair with Jenine?

MICKEY: No

They eat their ice lollies. She licks around hers with a long seductive tongue, then bites off abruptly.

LINDA: I make you feel lonely, don't I?

MICKEY: Yes

LINDA: (*She looks at him with a vast range of suppressed feelings passing across her face. She looks down, her eyes are full of a dishonest hatred she is unaware of.*) Sorry. (*She doesn't mean it but she thinks she does.*)

MICKEY: That's ok

LINDA: I just don't like it when you think I'm abnormal

MICKEY: How do you know I think you're abnormal

LINDA: Because I am. But if you were nice to me I'd be better

MICKEY: I am nice to you

LINDA: Never for long enough

MICKEY: Because you're never better for long enough

Pause.

LINDA: Tell me you love me

MICKEY: (*Turns to her. Opens his mouth, makes a series of dreadful grimaces but can make no words come out. He collapses in a faint. She looks down at him.*)

LINDA: It's alright for you, you've got somewhere else to go. I've got nothing. I'm all alone in a black pit of despair

MICKEY: (*On the ground, doesn't move. Opens one eye.*) You've got your father

LINDA: My father is darkness

MICKEY: I've dropped my Mivvi

LINDA: Have mine

MICKEY: Thanks. (*Doesn't move.*)

LINDA: Do you remember when we met?

MICKEY: Yep. (*Sits up. Takes her ice lolly.*)

LINDA: I was lovely

MICKEY: Yes, you were

LINDA: And still only a child. How you loved me then!

MICKEY: I still –

LINDA: What?

MICKEY: I still –

LINDA: Mickey, you're eating my Mivvi

MICKEY: I said, I still –

LINDA: Mickey, there's a spider on your face

MICKEY: It's a moth

LINDA: Why do you blame me for everything that's gone wrong?

MICKEY: Because it's all your fault

LINDA: Yes, you say that but I'm not sure I can believe it

MICKEY: You can't believe it? Well whose fault do you think it is then. Mine?

LINDA: No, no not yours – I didn't say that did I?

MICKEY: Don't look at me like that

LINDA: (*Stares at him.*)

MICKEY: Did you hear me?

LINDA: Yes

MICKEY: Stop it

LINDA: (*Shrinks from him.*)

MICKEY: (*He shrinks from her in imitation. Then rushes back at her.*) Don't shrink from me like that

LINDA: (*Staring.*) I didn't

MICKEY: You didn't

MR STEVENSON comes out of the house.

MR STEVENSON: Unhand my daughter this instant

MICKEY: Oh it's you. Why don't you do something about your daughter

MR STEVENSON: Don't you think I've tried? Sometimes I think if I had strength left in these hands I'd strangle the last breath out of her

MICKEY: What do you want out here? Why don't you go back to your..... and leave us alone

MR STEVENSON: I came to ask how long you intend to live in this house. The overcrowding is affecting my asthma

MICKEY: Not a moment longer

MR STEVENSON: Oh yes and where will you go, you're penniless. When I was your age, I had a string of attractive women to receive me

MICKEY: What makes you think I don't, eh?

MR STEVENSON: Your obvious relish for my daughter is proof enough. Why can't you find yourself a normal, healthy woman?

MICKEY: I've never met one

MR STEVENSON: Misogynist! You'll never touch my daughter again. What is this sticky mess I'm standing in?

MICKEY: That's my ice lolly

MR STEVENSON: Thank god. I thought it was one of Linda's calamities. Come inside for Christ's sake before the neighbours see us

*   *   *

A room, darkness. Persistent knocking on the door. Stops. Persistent knocking on the window. Hushed voices inside the room.

MICKEY: Open it

JENINE: I'm not opening it

Sound of a piece of coat hanger scraping around the window, itself behind drawn curtains.

MICKEY: She's trying to open the window

JENINE: What shall we do?

MICKEY: Don't move or she'll see you

JENINE: She's gone mad out there. Oh why didn't we open it?

MICKEY: It's too late now, here she comes

As the window is finally forced open a female figure leaps from a bed and scampers across the room in her underwear, and out. The curtains are suddenly torn down and another female figure emerges through the window, LINDA.

LINDA: That's charming. (*Steps onto a sofa then onto the floor, turns the light on.*)

MICKEY: (*Sitting on the bed wrapped in a blanket.*) Hello

LINDA: Where is she?

MICKEY: Who?

JENINE re-enters in her knickers.

JENINE: Hello Linda

LINDA: Thanks. (*To JENINE.*) Are you pregnant?

JENINE: No

LINDA: Why not?

JENINE: Because I'm not allowed to be

LINDA: So... Well I must say it feels different to actually see it

MICKEY: Where are my trousers?

LINDA: ... it makes me feel...

MICKEY: ... under the chair

LINDA: ... a bit sick

MICKEY: You always feel sick, twenty-four hours a day

LINDA: It's a nervous complaint, Mickey

MICKEY: Hand them to me Jenine

JENINE: Get them yourself

LINDA: I know what's going on now, don't I?

JENINE: Really? I wish you'd tell me

LINDA: Mickey knows... come on explain

MICKEY: ... I spend the whole time explaining

LINDA: ... light-hearted, aren't I?

MICKEY: ... in fact it's so long since I had an honest thought in my head...

LINDA: This won't do you any good

JENINE: (*Puts her coat on.*) You'll be torn in two forever

LINDA: You'll end up with neither

JENINE: You'll be lonely

LINDA: Leave her

JENINE: Leave her

MICKEY: Yes

LINDA: Which?

MICKEY: Yes, whichever

LINDA: If you have a child with her, you'll ruin my life

MICKEY: (*To JENINE.*) There, you see it's not possible

JENINE: A whole side of me has opened up like a trap, it's too late

MICKEY: Linda your shoes are digging into my trousers. If you lift your heel you will flick them over here to me

JENINE: ... and when you two have more children, where will that leave me?

MICKEY: Where?

JENINE: Standing in the kitchen in my knickers as always... I don't know why I'm hanging around

LINDA: No why are you?

JENINE: I suppose I'm hoping for my own good as well as his that he'll change his mind. (*Picks up the phone.*) Can I use it? I have to pick up Wilberforce from nursery

LINDA: Why not? Go on

JENINE: After all, you were always talking long distance on mine

LINDA: That was because I wasn't well

JENINE: And now I can't pay my bill

LINDA: Well? I'm sorry. (*To MICKEY.*) How do you think it feels to be called into question like this?

JENINE: Hello. Can I have a cab please, same address, yes. If it's cut off, I'll be isolated from all my friends because of you

MICKEY: She needs friends, Linda. Why did you do that?

LINDA: (*Not answering.*) It hurts

JENINE: You see, you'll be left with nothing. Make up your mind, I don't mind if it's her

MICKEY: Would someone give me my trousers

JENINE: Poor Linda. I love her too but I can still see what a terrible waste it all is. All we ever hear about is this fairy-tale romance and even I have been in love with it but now I'm sick of it. She gives you nothing and I'm bursting with so much I could give you, all you need but I won't ever be able to because I am second best and always have been

MICKEY: It's not like that. I love you, I love her

JENINE: You're driving me mad like you've driven her mad

MICKEY: Judas

JENINE: I know nothing is harder than to give her up but in losing the most you would gain the most. Nothing is easier than giving me up but in losing the least you will gain the least... why am I saying this?

MICKEY: Why are you saying this?

JENINE: Because I love you

LINDA: This has got to stop

MICKEY: I agree

LINDA: I'm beginning to realise how much damage all this has done to me

JENINE: I'm going, goodbye Linda

LINDA: (*Tears.*) Goodbye

JENINE: If it's any consolation, I'm going to hurt more than anyone because I'm the odd one out. (*They embrace then JENINE breaks from LINDA and moves to go.*) I want you to sell your motorbike

MICKEY: Why?

JENINE: You know why

LINDA: Why?

JENINE: Please Mickey, sell it, don't prevaricate, it would be cruel. I couldn't bear to think of you riding about on it without me. Goodbye

MICKEY: Sell it, yes, anything

JENINE: You can phone me if you need me, otherwise don't. (*Goes out.*)

LINDA walks out and away, hands dangling by her sides, leaving MICKEY standing alone. He puts his trousers on and puts his hand over his eyes like a visor, the other hand over his ear and stumbles about blindly. JENINE comes back into the room, MICKEY stares at her.

JENINE: What?

MICKEY: What?

JENINE: Leave me alone, will you please. You do understand that? Otherwise I'll be stuck like this forever... (*Pause.*)

MICKEY: Are you going to wait out there?

JENINE: For a little while, until the taxi comes. What are you going to do?

MICKEY shrugs.

Tell her you can't live without me

MICKEY: Yes, ok

JENINE: Don't do it because I tell you

MICKEY: No...

JENINE: Do it because... (*Pause.*) ... kiss me goodbye then

MICKEY kisses her, falls sleepily into her arms.

Don't go to sleep

*   *   *

A taxi arrives, door opens, closes. Taxi departs.

A few moments later JENINE walks slowly into view in front of the house dressed in a smart jacket with a neat skirt, hat, gloves and handbag. She walks up the steps to the door but changes her mind comes down and sits sedately on a garden chair, waits.

MICKEY comes out rubbing his eyes, stumbles and nearly falls down the steps.

JENINE: Did you tell her I was coming?

MICKEY: Why don't you go in and say hello?

JENINE: Who to?

MICKEY: I don't know, maybe the children will recognise you

JENINE: Is the taxi still there?

MICKEY: Go and look

JENINE stands up and goes out.

MICKEY picks up the chair she was sitting on and tries to smash it against the wall, throws the chair away.

LINDA comes out gasping for breath.

LINDA: For God's sake! Help me, Mickey! I can't get enough air indoors, quick, help me sit down. Where's that garden chair?

MICKEY: I don't know

LINDA: You've probably smashed it up. Go and find it

MICKEY takes a few blind steps in no direction.

LINDA sees JENINE who re-enters. LINDA composes herself.

LINDA: Beautiful this place of mine, isn't it? (*Sighs.*)

MICKEY returns to LINDA after staggering in a circle.

LINDA: (*To JENINE.*) Have you seen my chair?

JENINE: Mickey call another taxi

MICKEY: Call one yourself

LINDA: (*Distressed.*) My chair

JENINE: Where are my bags?

LINDA: Have you lost something?

JENINE: Yes, my luggage

LINDA: Mickey, find Jenine's luggage

MICKEY: The taxi drove off with it

JENINE: Mickey, I'm leaving. Call a taxi

MICKEY: (*Ignores the order.*) Bye bye, Linda love

LINDA: Bye Mickey. Jenine's confused, Mickey

JENINE: Why are you here, Linda?

LINDA: I got the days muddled up. What are you here for?
I think it's tragic the way your friendship is going to be
sacrificed for all this... where are you going?

JENINE: Where, Mickey?

MICKEY: We're going to the The.

LINDA: to the...??

MICKEY: Linda, shut up, shut up. Mind your own business

LINDA: Jenine, do you want to go dancing, tomorrow?

JENINE: With you?

LINDA: Yes, dancing. (*She demonstrates.*)

MICKEY: Linda, could you go inside

LINDA: (*She goes up the steps.*) Alright, Mickey

JENINE: Yes, I'd like to

LINDA: Alright then. (*As she goes in.*)

MICKEY: (*Pause.*) Who was that on the swing, just now?

JENINE: (*Goes over to the swing.*) I was

> *A baby starts crying inside the house. LINDA comes out aimlessly down
> the steps. Pause. They all stare at each other.*

LINDA: Mickey, do you know why the baby is crying?

JENINE: Christ...

MICKEY: Is it?

LINDA: (*To MICKEY.*) What's the matter?

MICKEY: Is the baby crying?

JENINE: Linda

LINDA: Yes?

JENINE: What's the matter darling?

LINDA: Mickey, would you?

MICKEY: No

LINDA: Jenine, where's your baggage?

JENINE: In the taxi, apparently

LINDA: Stop that fucking baby!

MICKEY: (*Blind.*) Where is it?

LINDA: Indoors! It's indoors somewhere!

MICKEY: Point me at the steps

JENINE: What are you doing, Mickey, stop it!

MICKEY: Linda, help me, I can't see

JENINE: Of course he can

MICKEY: Linda, help me

LINDA: What's wrong with him?

JENINE: Mickey

   MICKEY falls on his face. Doesn't move.

JENINE: Mickey, I'm going

MICKEY: No...

JENINE: Yes, listen, I'll come and visit you

MICKEY: No, don't leave me here

LINDA: What's the matter? Mickey, you're so... oh I don't know

MICKEY: Tell her to stop, I'm not well

JENINE: You're fine, stand up

MICKEY: Please don't

LINDA: Don't touch him, Jenine

JENINE: But Linda

LINDA: No, because you know why, I caught you together, didn't I? So don't touch him

JENINE: (*Gets up, steps back.*) Alright

LINDA: Do you think it strange my dad deals with the baby crying?

JENINE: Lovely. I don't care

LINDA: Why not?

JENINE: It's not my baby

LINDA: But you'd like it to be?

MICKEY: Linda, I think I know where your chair is

LINDA: Don't start that Mickey now

MICKEY: Christ knows we all need a sit down every now and again

LINDA: You might

MICKEY: I do, yes

JENINE: Can you dance, Linda?

LINDA: Yes, I'm very sexy

MICKEY: – except she's got little piggy eyes

LINDA: You can't see my eyes because I close them

MICKEY: Shifty pools of piss

LINDA: Don't spoil it Mickey

MICKEY: It gives me the creeps just looking at you

LINDA: What's the matter with me?

MICKEY: I think it must be your body language, love...

LINDA: Oh

MICKEY: ... reminds me of a trip to the cemetery

LINDA: Oh...

MICKEY: ... that and your face...

LINDA: ... anything else?

MICKEY: ... nothing, except you bore me rigid

LINDA: ... I know...

MICKEY: ... and everyone else

LINDA: I don't think so

MICKEY: Ask anyone, if you can keep their attention long enough

LINDA: (*To JENINE.*) He's so rude, isn't he?

JENINE: I'm just a weapon between you, aren't I Mickey?

MICKEY: Look at her

JENINE: (*Looks at LINDA.*)

LINDA: (*Looks at JENINE, a weak smile endeavouring to hide her anger.*)

MICKEY: Who wants to be looked at like that?

JENINE: Let's arrange another day

MICKEY: Do you want me to stay and look after you Linda?

LINDA: (*Cries.*) Yes

MICKEY: Alright, I'll go and get my cudgel

LINDA: (*Looks at him, uncomprehending.*)

MICKEY: My cudgel, I said

LINDA: (*Stares at him, frozen.*)

MICKEY: (*Raises his fist at her.*) My cudgel

LINDA: (*Tears.*)

JENINE turns and leaves. LINDA and MICKEY go inside. Night falls, time passes.

*   *   *

Day breaks.

LINDA, MICKEY and MR STEVENSON come out of the house into the garden. MR STEVENSON stands superciliously regarding his borders.

MICKEY: I bet he's had his finger in your pie

MR STEVENSON: Does he know how depressed I am Linda?

MICKEY: ... I can see

MR STEVENSON: Wait until Sunday, my breath falls into the wall and my eyes weeping like a liquor still...

MICKEY: I won't make it to Sunday at this rate

MR STEVENSON: Oh, have you lost your love?

MICKEY: I've lost two. They warned me...

MR STEVENSON: You see, he's fallen under my charm

LINDA: Why are all these leaves still lying on the floor, why?

MR STEVENSON: Yes, they do drive us back upon our memories, don't they?

MICKEY: Why what?

LINDA: All you've done is lie to me for years, I think you've taken advantage of me

MR STEVENSON: Yes, you've availed yourself of her weakness, young man. Her weakness in the head, like an egg, unbroken and yet rancid inside. Oh how can I be happy? The girl cries beside me in bed at night. It's very upsetting, we're both asleep; but sleep – ? Wait until after dinner, I could thrust you all apart. All this standing staring... you're all mad. Is there someone outside my garden?

LINDA: Is she outside?

MR STEVENSON: (*To himself. Scratching a flea indignantly.*) What's going on...

MICKEY: Who?

LINDA: I thought I saw her

MICKEY: No, I can't see anyone

LINDA: How long will this go on, I can't get her out of my mind

Every time I look at you, she's behind you. She hates me now, at last openly hates me, she wishes I would drown

A knock at the garden gate.

MR STEVENSON: At last my taxi has arrived

LINDA: You're not going anywhere, Daddy. (*Goes to look.*) It's her

MICKEY: Unlock the gate then, blimey

MR STEVENSON: Me? I wouldn't know what to say.

LINDA: She must be protected from all pain, while I... (*Sighs.*) ... I am not to be protected. Why?

Because I'm the winner

MR STEVENSON: My daughter? The winner? I never allowed it

LINDA: The loser has come round to gloat

MR STEVENSON: It must be the taxi I think, pardon me please

MICKEY: Stop edging forward, get back

MR STEVENSON: Don't stop me please. Youth, Ah!

Gate opens. JENINE steps in, smiles at MICKEY, stands by the gate, opens her handbag.

Silence.

LINDA: What's she doing here?

MR STEVENSON: Now, now, now, if a beautiful girl wants to mount the steps to my house...

JENINE: Hello Mickey

MR STEVENSON: Who is she? Has she come to announce something?

JENINE: I saw your children outside playing...

MICKEY: (*Interrupting. To MR STEVENSON.*) Your taxi has arrived

MR STEVENSON: But I'm not going anywhere

JENINE: (*To LINDA.*) Don't look at me like that. People always want what they can't have, while at the same time they destroy what they were attracted to. How are you?

LINDA: Much better, yes much better. I'm better you know, whereas you, I can see, you're much worse. Oh you're so much worse. Nothing has helped you

JENINE: (*Bows head politely. Smiles.*)

LINDA: We're rich now, money came from nowhere

JENINE: Yes, we're all a shade better than we used to be

LINDA: Even Mickey

JENINE: Yes?

LINDA: Have you seen the way he stumbles about though?

JENINE: And does he still have a constant fever?

LINDA: All that shaking and gasping?

MR STEVENSON: Is this his lover? Her breasts are smaller than I imagined

MICKEY: She breast-fed too long

JENINE: Does he still say he's a genius?

LINDA: He tries to explain that to me, but I don't understand

JENINE: You never listened

LINDA: Only because I knew you would

JENINE: Every word fell like gold coins into my heart...

LINDA: And now, how is your heart?

JENINE: Open

LINDA: Isn't the world cruel

JENINE: Yes, but I'm free to enjoy it

MR STEVENSON: I'm surprised by your appearance madam; Linda, how could you have competed with this lovely girl, she wins my heart immediately

MICKEY: Isn't she lovely?

MR STEVENSON: Do you know my dear, my heart is full of stones? My daughter won t respond to my caresses

JENINE just smiles, holds her ground.

MR STEVENSON: Isn't she strong

LINDA: Yes, what a performance. Mickey, I don't feel very well

MICKEY goes to her but MR STEVENSON stands in the way.

LINDA: Mickey

MICKEY: What's wrong Linda?

LINDA: Sickness. (*She turns away.*)

MR STEVENSON: Get a bowl for her then

MICKEY: (*Holds out his hands and she is sick into them.*) Jenine pass me a tissue

JENINE stands motionless.

MR STEVENSON: (*Pours sherry into a glass, hands it to LINDA.*) And look, look what we're drinking here, Linda is used to this aren't you lovey?

JENINE: What's the matter with her?

MR STEVENSON: It's morning sickness I think

LINDA: Mickey I want to go behind a tree

MICKEY: Hang on, one minute, just one minute

LINDA: Mickey

MICKEY: One minute, just one minute

LINDA: ... what are you waiting for?

MICKEY: I don't know

JENINE: Oh for god's sake

MR STEVENSON: Yes, it's morning sickness I think

JENINE: Is she pregnant then?

MR STEVENSON: I don't know, is she pregnant, Mick?

MICKEY: Is she what?

JENINE: (*Angry.*) Why didn't you tell me?

MICKEY: She...

JENINE: That's it, that's bloody it

LINDA: (*Vomits.*)

MR STEVENSON: (*Politely.*) Have you seen this sort of thing before?

JENINE: (*Sits on a garden chair in tears.*) You bastard

MICKEY: Don't cry. (*Puts his arm around her shoulder and strokes her head.*) My flaxen-haired angel...

JENINE: How could you let it happen before I had time to prepare myself?

LINDA: (*From behind a tree.*) Mickey...

MICKEY: Where is she?

MR STEVENSON: She's popped behind the tree there

MICKEY limps blindly across.

MR STEVENSON: (*Goes to sit down painfully on a garden chair.*) Oh, oh, oh, oh, oh, oh, help me love here will you, my coccyx isn't straight, a cushion

JENINE shoves a cushion under without turning to look.

MICKEY: What the hell's wrong with her?

MR STEVENSON: Little slut, she's always been like it. Ate nothing but spaghetti as a child, and now look at her...

JENINE: (*Stands. Closes handbag.*) Right

MICKEY: What?

JENINE: What's the matter with her, you must know

MICKEY: I don't know

JENINE: (*Shakes her head.*)

LINDA: (*Weakly from behind the tree.*) Mickey

JENINE: Well...

MICKEY sits on chair blindly.

MR STEVENSON: (*Stands up.*) Oh, are you going? A shame. My daughter you know, she's very... have you a career?

JENINE: Me? No. Why don't you attend to her?

MR STEVENSON: (*Standing stock still, staring at JENINE.*) I will, I will as the Lord is my witness

JENINE walks in smart shoes and clothes away.

MR STEVENSON: Goodbye my pretty

Clip clop of JENINE's shoes, LINDA rustles from behind the tree.

MR STEVENSON: There is a bit of conflict

MICKEY: We're all friends

MR STEVENSON: Your life is rather small I note

MICKEY: ... It's getting smaller

*   *   *

LINDA and MR STEVENSON in a room. LINDA yawns.

MR STEVENSON: I don't mind you sleeping, sleep, sleep

LINDA: It's alright

MR STEVENSON: I just wish you wouldn't yawn while I'm talking

LINDA: You weren't talking

MR STEVENSON: No, God bless you

Pause.

Watch over me tonight

LINDA: Yes

MR STEVENSON: Am I asking too much? I will take a short walk. Don't follow this time, it's unlikely I will do anything foolish. (*He stumbles to the door, tries to open it but can't. He falls back weakly.*) No, no, I can't, you see

LINDA stands and drags herself to the door.

You see, you open the door for me... without you how would I...

LINDA: (*Tries the handle but it breaks off.*) It's broken.

MR STEVENSON: ... find the beauty that waits for me outside or, being alone, how would I –

Returns and stands beside the mattress.

Will you sleep now?

LINDA looks towards the window.

Sleep now, sleep, I'm nodding off myself. These long summer evenings, no-one around, I have nothing to think of...

something was mine, someone...

never fear, I will always pause beside you... you are my daughter

LINDA sleeps on the mattress.

He goes to the door and rattles what's left of the handle.

LINDA: (*Talking in her sleep.*) Daddy, Daddy! there's someone holding onto my arm

MR STEVENSON: Impossible, you are sleeping so peacefully...

LINDA: Let go, let go

MR STEVENSON: (*Approaches the mattress.*) Hello, little creature, who can you be? Faceless baby sitting on the end of the bed...

LINDA: Daddy, it hasn't got a face

MR STEVENSON: (*Goes and stands by her feet.*) Come on little baby let me pick you up in my arms, no I never cared for you before but now, hup, heyhup. (*He lifts a black shape from the end of the bed.*)

LINDA: It won't let go. (*To the black shape.*)

MR STEVENSON: There, there, little baby, come to the corner with me

LINDA: Daddy

MR STEVENSON: We'll see the little duckies and the pond. (*Goes to the door with the black shape in his arms. Stands facing the door he can't open.*) I can't see past my own failure

LINDA sleeps peacefully.

MR STEVENSON goes back to the bed.

Linda, I can't get out. I'd like to see my garden, it's so beautiful in the summer... get up, there's strength in you yet to help me

(*She gets up.*)

and when I've gone, you can rest

MICKEY arrives outside the bedroom door and rattles the handle.

MICKEY: Linda, let me in

MR STEVENSON: Who is it?

MICKEY: Open up old man

MR STEVENSON: What for?

MICKEY: What for, well it isn't so I can see your silly smile. I live here

MR STEVENSON: No you don't

MICKEY: Where's Linda?

MR STEVENSON: She's here, she's sleep-walking at the moment. It's most inconvenient, she can't see you

MICKEY bursts open the door.

You see, she doesn't know you

MICKEY: You're quite right, never mind, since she's up I'll have her bed, you keep watch

MR STEVENSON: I can't I'm too infirm. I'm afraid of the dark. I'll have no truck with these dreams of hers. She only does it to insult me. Take her off my hands

MICKEY: I'm not nursing your offspring mate

MR STEVENSON: I'm begging you. I can't bear her silent criticisms any more. We've all made mistakes but she persecutes me. I've a good few years left in me yet, I'd like to live them in peace

Pause.

MICKEY: What a hoax

MR STEVENSON: You're right my boy. I won't let you lay a finger on her, I was merely hoping for a small contribution to her psychiatric bills

MICKEY: Forget it

MR STEVENSON: What were you expecting? Some charmer I'll wager to sweeten the bitter pill of your miserable life. Well my daughter I'll have you know has more infirmities than the buttons on your coat

LINDA falls slowly to the ground, asleep.

These fainting fits for example, who better than her father to pass the pillow under her head?

MICKEY: (*Smiles.*) You've got a nice little thing going

MR STEVENSON: You admit it?

MICKEY: I'll admit anything if you let me get some sleep

MR STEVENSON: Go ahead, try all you like. Sleep is a stranger to this room

*   *   *

In the woods beside a lake.

MICKEY: Let's pretend we're happy beside a lake somewhere. Ducks and geese migrate overhead... the children...

(*Children's laughter.*) ... are happily playing in the water

MICKEY sits happily on the ground, his shirt sleeves and trousers rolled up.

CHILD'S VOICE: (*Off.*) Watch me dancing, watch me dancing!

MICKEY: (*To LINDA over by the basket.*) Bring over some lemonade, let's have some lemonade

LINDA prepares some lemonade.

(*To JENINE.*) Sit down here beside me, ooh we're such old lovers aren't we love?

JENINE: (*Awkward silence.*)

MICKEY: What's wrong?

JENINE: (*No reply.*)

MICKEY: Not that old stuff again?

JENINE: (*Tears.*) I don't know why

MICKEY: Oh well, come one, come on, watch the child dancing then... (*Watches her face.*) you can't even manage that can you?

JENINE stares frozen with fear at where the child's voice comes from.

Come on, you'll disappoint the kid... stop thinking about yourself, no one's watching you

LINDA: (*Calling from the table.*) Mickey, there's flies in the lemonade

MICKEY: It doesn't matter

CHILD'S VOICE: (*Off.*) Mummy, I'm falling!

JENINE: Wait darling, mummy's coming (*But she's still frozen.*)

MICKEY: (*Turns and stares at JENINE's frozen face.*) Boo! (*He gets up.*) Linda, where's that fucking lemonade?

LINDA: I spilled it...

MICKEY: You what?

LINDA: No, here's some on the table. (*She reaches for a cup.*)

MICKEY: (*Turns again to JENINE.*) Please don't stand there

JENINE: Mickey

MICKEY: Don't, with that shawl around your face, I can't see you

JENINE: I'm sorry

LINDA: Here Mickey. (*Goes to hand him a cup of lemonade but knocks it over on the table.*)

MICKEY: Mind that cup, mind it, mind it, mind it! (*In a rage he tips the table over.*)

LINDA freezes.

Everything you do is so invisible, no one else can see it, but I can see it!

LINDA: No, Mickey

MICKEY: Why do you keep dropping that cup?

LINDA: I think it's because you react in this way

MICKEY: Hadn't someone better fish Wilberforce out of the lake?

JENINE stands up, rooted to the spot.

MICKEY goes off to the side.

LINDA hands JENINE some lemonade.

LINDA: Hadn't you better go?

JENINE: What?

LINDA: And fish out Wilberforce

JENINE: Mickey's doing it, isn't he?

LINDA: Do you trust him?

JENINE: He's the only man I would trust alone with my children

MICKEY comes back.

MICKEY: There, I've drowned the little bugger. (*Goes to the picnic hamper.*)

LINDA: (*To JENINE.*) I see. (*Walks apart.*)

MICKEY: (*To JENINE, who wraps herself in her shawl.*) I see you're not your witty intelligent self, these days

JENINE: I told you it would happen, it's your own fault

MICKEY: (*To LINDA.*) I've lost her to the ravages of the mind as well. Did you bring any drumsticks?

LINDA: I forgot

MICKEY: (*To JENINE.*) Stop crying

JENINE: It's what I'm here for. Otherwise I could be in the fields under a blue sky in the sun with your baby

LINDA: Tell her to –

MICKEY: Pardon Linda. (*Puts his hand up to his ear.*) I can't hear you

LINDA: Tell her to shut up

JENINE: If I fell into a puddle I wouldn't make a splash. If you cut out my heart and fed it to the turtle dove that circles above us, I wouldn't murmur

> *LINDA violently tips the contents of the hamper onto the ground.*

If you laid upon me and stifled me I wouldn't gasp except with love... all this I'd give you

MICKEY: (*Picks out food from the mess.*) You've broken all the bloody plates

JENINE: If only you'd stand and, and leave your soul behind...

MICKEY: (*To LINDA, snatching a small sandwich.*) Give me that

JENINE: I'd help you build a new one, I have your soul firmly in mind, in my breasts, there's your new soul

MICKEY: (*To LINDA.*) What's the matter aren't you going to eat or something?

LINDA: I've lost my appetite

MICKEY: (*To BOTH.*) Excuse me is this meant to be a picnic or not?

JENINE looks at him sympathetically, he catches her eye.

And some friend you are

JENINE: You haven't got any friends Mickey

MICKEY: I've got you

JENINE: I'm not a friend any more

MICKEY: Well

JENINE: But just because it's possible to forget someone doesn't mean you ought to, does it?

LINDA stamps on some plates and food.

MICKEY: (*Pushes her out of the way.*) Excuse me I want the mustard. (*Goes into a rage.*) Where is it? (*In a hysterical frenzy he kicks the remains of the picnic to pieces.*)

LINDA: You always have to be angrier than me

MICKEY: (*Ferocious.*) What?

LINDA: (*Intimidated.*) You –

MICKEY: I'm not angry, I'm looking for the bloody mustard. (*He sets off one hand over his eyes the other held to his ear.*)

LINDA: Where are you going?

MICKEY: For a ride

LINDA: When will you be back?

MICKEY: Soon

JENINE: Are you going on your motorbike?

MICKEY: Yes

JENINE: I thought you were selling it?

MICKEY: I am

JENINE: When?

MICKEY: Soon, now if you like, just let me know

JENINE: I'm jealous, I'm hurt

MICKEY: So am I

JENINE: I can't sleep

MICKEY: Neither can I

LINDA: Neither can I

MICKEY: We'll all be fine

JENINE: Can't you walk instead?

MICKEY: Would you like to come on the back?

LINDA: You two can't go off together like that

JENINE: Those days are gone Mickey, don't you understand?

MICKEY: (*To LINDA.*) You come then

JENINE: Mickey!

MICKEY: Alright I'll go on my own

JENINE: Sell it

MICKEY: It's as good as sold. Where's my helmet?

MICKEY wanders off.

JENINE: (*To LINDA.*) Love is like a poison isn't it?

LINDA: What?

*   *   *

A park, ducks, a pond nearby.

The wind blows, whistles sadly.

MICKEY wanders into view. He wears a plastic visor above his eyes, jeans, trainers and a begrimed anorak-like waistcoat with the stars and stripes pattern on it. He carries a plastic bag with contents.

MICKEY: (*Looking around in the distance.*) Who's here?

He approaches a mound of damp clothes lying on the grass.

Why are you left? Where is your house, you had a house. (*He moves the clothes with his foot.*)

He sets off again, a shadow of a man walks across the wall, a small dog follows him on a lead, he recedes into the distance shrinking.

LINDA runs up the green hill after him, stumbling in her high heels.

LINDA: Mickey!

He doesn't turn round.

Mickey (*She starts crying.*) don't go!

MICKEY: (*Turns and hides his plastic bag.*) I'm not

LINDA: Don't leave me

MICKEY: I'm only going for a walk

LINDA: No, Mickey Mickey, I love you! (*She runs up to him her face red and swelling with tears.*) My lovely boy, I can't believe it! What's happening?

MICKEY: I don't know

LINDA: It's like a nightmare, help me!

MICKEY: I can't

LINDA: It's all just gone, I'm empty like a shell, take me with you

MICKEY: (*Laughs.*) I can't very well do that can I love?

They laugh, she cries.

MICKEY: Please

LINDA: Is this the moment then?

MICKEY: Yes...

LINDA: No... (*She reaches out to him.*)

MICKEY: (*Shakes his head, almost shrugs his shoulders, turns.*)

LINDA: No! (*Cries.*)

MICKEY: (*Turns back.*) What?

LINDA: Where will you go?

He walks.

MR STEVENSON appears.

LINDA: Wait, Mickey, here's Dad

MR STEVENSON comes.

Dad look there's Mickey

MR STEVENSON: Hello Mick

MICKEY keeps going.

LINDA: (*Catches MICKEY, brings him back.*) Here's Mickey Dad

MR STEVENSON: Hello Mick... What's wrong with Mickey Linda?

LINDA: He's leaving me Dad

MR STEVENSON: What Mick?

MICKEY: Yes

MR STEVENSON: Goodbye Mick. Peter lifted up his hand like this and said: The Lord is Love

MICKEY: Yes

MR STEVENSON: The Lord is Love Mickey

MICKEY: Yes

MR STEVENSON: Are you leaving Linda pregnant?

MICKEY: (*Walks backwards, laughs a bit.*) Sure

MR STEVENSON: (*To LINDA.*) I can't think of your mother without going into a rage... I've got to finish it, I've got to finish it I said to myself, I sat at home waiting for her, 'come home' like that 'come home' because I knew I had to finish it... I think she was betraying me

LINDA: Mickey

MR STEVENSON: Was she do you think?

LINDA: Oh!

MR STEVENSON: Whore!

LINDA: Don't call her that

MR STEVENSON: I'm sorry, Mick, Linda's crying, comfort her

LINDA: I'm not

MR STEVENSON: She's been crying. You look after her, look after the women here, and all the babies and try to give up smoking, I'm going off now to have some fun, leave all the little ladies behind

Why did she always let the loonies inside her house?

MICKEY: I don't know

MR STEVENSON: Yes, I'm sorry Mick, nothing personal, you wouldn't like that lot from the day centre in your house either would you?

MICKEY moves off.

MR STEVENSON: (*Calls after him.*) And your old Mum and Dad

MICKEY: What about them?

MR STEVENSON: Let them die in peace, pile coats on top of them when it gets cold, that's all they ask

LINDA: Mickey I love you!... What about all the abortions I've had

MICKEY: What about them?

LINDA: Don't you think that ought to make you feel a bit of responsibility?

MICKEY: It's a free country

MR STEVENSON: Mick, tell her you love her, you'll do anything for her, win her back

MICKEY goes.

Has he gone?

LINDA: Yes

MR STEVENSON: Forever do you think? (*Smiles.*)

End of Part One.

PART TWO

MICKEY: (*Staggers forward.*) I have returned (*Sits on the floor, stands.*)

Friends? (*Laughs.*) They're here somewhere... Where I don't know... (*Looks about blindly.*)

This life...

Right this is it, I'm going to bust this thing now (*Calls.*) I'm home!... Oh forget it (*Turns, faints, unconscious.*)

LINDA comes in wheeling an empty pushchair.

Sounds of children aged 2 or 3, sound stops.

She calls her children after her.

LINDA: (*Lazily.*) Come on

(*Kind and coaxing.*) Come on

She rolls a cigarette, holds it smiles ahead of her.

MICKEY stands.

MICKEY: I have returned

He walks away stiffly, blindly, listing to the left his hand up to his eyes like a vizor.

LINDA: I'm over here

MICKEY: (*Stops.*) Don't look at me while I'm dreaming it spoils the effect

LINDA: Mickey, Mickey I'm here

MICKEY: Give us a break please; there's a bloke down the road...

LINDA: What bloke?

MICKEY: In fact there's a load of blokes down the road...
(*Laughs.*)

LINDA: Come on darlings, come to mummy (*She turns about her, the children aren't there.*)

MICKEY: It is the mother... a world of things picking at the children... defenceless

LINDA: Hurry up loves

MICKEY: Where's...

LINDA: Mickey

MICKEY: ... Peter Piper?

LINDA: Let's go inside...

MICKEY: No.

Where's the girl?

LINDA: Listen Mickey, Please...

MICKEY: I came back

LINDA: Mickey come here, come here, I want to whisper you something

MICKEY: No

LINDA: Come on... I'm going to a party

MICKEY: Look, whoever you are –

LINDA: Want to...? (*Gestures rudely.*)

MICKEY moves blindly to the pushchair.

(*Stops him.*) Mickey, Mickey, tell you what... I'm not wearing a bra

MICKEY: Got no tits

LINDA: Like a boy

MICKEY: Would you crawl in the other direction, I'm attending to my children... Hello babies...

LINDA: You've been gone, I've got myself a bald man with a motorbike. He gives it to me from –

MICKEY: So what? So have I, he lets me kick it when I'm blue (*Moves nearer to the pushchair. Listens.*) What was that?

LINDA: (*Listens.*)

MICKEY: A fart from far off. (*While she is distracted by this remark he stumbles the remaining steps to the pushchair and boots it so it flies across the ground.*)

LINDA makes to stop him but it's too late.

(*Smiles at her.*) A dog barks, the wind blows it away.......
What about this party then? Are we abnormal or something, no-one invites us

LINDA: You haven't been around

MICKEY: Don't tell me you've got friends, I'm your only fucking friend. Where are the children?

LINDA: They are stars in the sky

MICKEY: Very funny. (*Laughs.*)

LINDA: I wrote you a poem

MICKEY: I thought I could smell piss in your knickers

LINDA: That's because I love you

MICKEY holds one hand to his ear as if he's holding earphones, with the other he makes a vizor for his blind eyes, he sinks within himself.

Warm isn't it, for evening. And we're all dusty and dirty. I took the kiddies for a walk to the playground, feed the ducks: stupid ducks, they ate a whole wonderloaf and started sinking

MICKEY is still listening to the imaginary music in his imaginary headphones.

Then one of the other kids in the park picked up a johnny and put it in his mouth

MICKEY: (*Still headphones, he whispers softly, then louder.*) Crash, crash, crash, crash!

LINDA: His mum went spare

MICKEY: Kaboom! (*Nods.*) Listen, listen

The engine of a large motorbike far off.

LINDA: What's that?

MICKEY: Me arriving. Broom, Broom! (*He plays at riding a motorcycle, a broad grimace on his face. He suddenly weakens, a cold nausea destroys him, he fades to nothing, then returns with borrowed strength.*) How's your daddy?

LINDA: He's –

MICKEY: I hope you don't let your old daddy kiss your bum when you walk past his dying bed

LINDA: I smooth his pillow for him

MICKEY: I'll smooth his pillow for him

LINDA: (*Slinks up to him.*) Mickey...

MICKEY: You may as well keep it, I'm only here to celebrate...

LINDA: Yeah? What is there to celebrate?

MICKEY: In 1953 a little thing happened – I was born.

LINDA: 1953? You're too young

MICKEY: That's the modern world, you're too young, too old, too black too white, too fucking lazy. Get me a bottle

LINDA: Can't you do it in a corner?

MICKEY: A corner? I couldn't find a corner

LINDA: I'll show you

MICKEY: Let me in...

LINDA: No, Mickey

MICKEY: Why not? Don't you think I came all this way
to see you? I've even got you a present. Look, look here,
(*Searches his pockets.*) here's some... What do you want?...
I couldn't keep away to tell you the truth, wondering
where you were, what you were doing

LINDA: I see

MICKEY: Tell you the truth your well known hospitality
was eating up my bollocks. Point me to the door

LINDA: (*Points away.*) There

MICKEY: Liar. (*Walks blindly in the opposite direction towards
the house.*)

LINDA: Mickey I want to make this as painless as possible

MICKEY: Yeah?

LINDA: So I won't let you come in

MICKEY: Look, there's your daddy reading the headlines

LINDA: You can't see him he's on a mattress

MICKEY: Always on a mattress your dad, bed sores, worms
in his ears the whole lot

LINDA: Yeah and so have I, even the kiddies, so, we've got
enough trouble. All you care about is the state of my
private parts

MICKEY: There's nothing private there my dear..... You
don't understand the love of the mature man, it's...

getting to know them and watching them suffer it's a deep love of all human kind

LINDA: You don't love *me* then?

MICKEY: I love... your sad, dull, painful life my dear

LINDA: It sounds really good Mickey

MICKEY: Look, let's get it moving: How are you? Nice? What've you been doing? I hope you haven't had too much leisure time

LINDA: Why not?

MICKEY: I know what you do with it, on your back, legs in the air... is that why your thing always smells like a bath mat? Is it? Let me stay...

LINDA: I've really got to go now, nice of you to call round

MICKEY: Come on Linda (*He puts his hand around her thigh and squeezes until it hurts her.*)

LINDA: Ow!

MICKEY: (*Still gripping.*) Don't walk off. Go on feel that. We go to the pictures, no money, no money, but I'm happy, we are happy, we love each other, we are brothers, sisters

LINDA bites her lip in pain.

MICKEY: (*Lets go.*) Ah Linda, I cannot match your love... But I'll be a cousin to you, you can wash my shoes in the tumble drier, and I'll do you a few favours in return – fair? Ok

He falls to the ground.

LINDA: Christ Mickey (*Hobbles a few steps away, limping from a deadened thigh.*) What's the matter?

Silence.

Mickey?

Sound of a motorbike crashing nearby.

LINDA limps to where the pushchair is and picks it up.

MICKEY rolls onto his back.

I'm sorry Mickey, it's party time for me, all my friends...
They're waiting for me. I'll change when I get there...
In fact I won't bother... I like a drink though, cor yeah...
Come back any time, kiddies love a daddy. I nearly
forgot my poem, here it is:

> Mickey
> Got Sticky
> In his little Dicky
> Who put the scratch
> In my snatch

Why don't you clap?

MICKEY: I've only got the one working arm

LINDA walks off calling her children.

LINDA: Darlings, little loves

MICKEY squats shivering.

*MR STEVENSON comes in with a heavy stick. He sees MICKEY
and approaches from behind shaking and shuddering with effort and
rage. He raises his stick to strike at MICKEY's head.*

MICKEY: (*Looking up.*) Oh. Who are you waving to?

MR STEVENSON lowers his stick, walks away.

(*Getting to his feet.*) I was just saying to your daughter....

MR STEVENSON: Go away...

MICKEY: I have returned

MR STEVENSON: Welcome

MICKEY: (*His hand like a vizor, the other outstretched to feel.*)

MR STEVENSON: I must return to my mattress

MICKEY: I was just saying to your daughter –

MR STEVENSON: Do you mind, we're expecting visitors

MICKEY: Let's be friends shall we?

MR STEVENSON: No, please try to understand

Enter LINDA dressed for a party possibly.

LINDA: What do you think Mickey?

MICKEY: (*To MR STEVENSON.*) Where's...?

MR STEVENSON: She's not well

LINDA: Mickey, my dress...

MICKEY: (*Indicates LINDA.*) Poor cow eh?

MR STEVENSON: (*Looks at MICKEY.*)

LINDA: Mickey, my dress...

MICKEY: I can't bloody see it can I?

LINDA: Let's go

MICKEY: (*To MR STEVENSON.*) You think *I* gave her a hard time?

MR STEVENSON: Linda, I'm going inside, close all the doors, bolt the windows

LINDA: I'm sick of it

MR STEVENSON: One last time, please here take my elbow

LINDA: Mickey, take a taxi, in a few moments we'll be free, no-one will find us

MICKEY: I don't know of a rank, my arms won't lift and I can't whistle

LINDA: Here take my hand

Does so.

There. Doesn't that make you feel as if you could do anything you liked?

MICKEY: Did I tell you there's something wrong with your daughter?

MR STEVENSON: Linda I shall die if you don't help me

MICKEY: I'm off

MR STEVENSON: At least guide me to the door... I made you unhappy, and who has made me unhappy?

LINDA: I know a party we can go to

MICKEY: Sorry love, I left my tutu in the casualty ward

LINDA: We can have fun like we used to

MR STEVENSON: Welcome home my boy, welcome home

MICKEY: Well I'm not staying

MR STEVENSON: Come inside...

MICKEY: Stop staring at me Linda

LINDA: I can't help it

MR STEVENSON: ... and leave the wicked world outside, a child of mine needn't concern herself with the world at large. Cruel beasts wander and..... a child of mine... you understand Mick

A door slams.

Doors slam rudely in the wind. What did I achieve? I count my friends on one hand...

MICKEY walks off blindly.

MR STEVEN SON: (*Seizes MICKEY by the arm and won't let go.*)
And there'll only be one car in my funeral procession...
Mick, wait for me I'll come with you

LINDA: Mickey wait

MICKEY: I'm not going anywhere!

MR STEVENSON: Take care of your things Linda,
remember to switch off the oven, have you harmed the
baby today, something you said? You should be careful.
Have you ever thought, the damage we do to our children

LINDA: Take me away from it Mickey I can't stand it
any more

MICKEY: Well Mr Stevenson, how about a cup of tea?

MR STEVENSON: Certainly my boy, certainly

They walk towards the house together.

You want to come in for it I expect... yes, yes... You've
been gone a long time, why come back at all... you don't
mind me asking?

They disappear inside.

LINDA: Stop, get out of my house, get out!

JENINE approaches.

JENINE: (*She puts her arm around LINDA.*) You look so small,
it doesn't matter what they do, you're right not to let
them in

LINDA: Jenine

JENINE: Do you want me to help you? I've got nothing
to do this morning. Shall I baby-sit or something. Look
I brought this (*Takes out a child's pullover from a plastic bag.*)
yesterday for...

LINDA: Where did you get it?

JENINE: I bought it

LINDA: Did you? You found it?

JENINE: No, I bought it

LINDA: Where did you find it?

JENINE: I didn't find it

LINDA: It's been used

JENINE: I got it in a shop

LINDA: Why don't you say you found it?

JENINE: I bought it. I don't care

LINDA: I do

JENINE: Why? It doesn't matter

LINDA: You found it

JENINE: Somewhere

LINDA: Why not just say?

JENINE: I did. It doesn't matter

LINDA: Thanks anyway, it's nice, nice colours, bit warm
    for the summer

JENINE: Linda, lend me five pounds, I've got to have five
    pounds I've got no cigs

LINDA: (*Puts hat on.*) You spend all your time begging
    cigarettes

JENINE: Yes, it's so degrading, you know I'm really
    educated, they think I'm a tart but really... keep the cigs.
    Please help me. You do trust me don't you? Why are you
    sad today?...

LINDA: I have to be alone Jenine

JENINE: *I* have to be alone, I have to get away, they
want to give me electric shocks. That won't cure me
because there's nothing wrong with me, I just need a
lot of money and good living, I was born to it, I was
adopted by the wrong people, I needed people with
class, anyway give me £5 and I'll tidy up here for
you, you look so lonely, I know how it feels. I've
been lonely. You go and sleep and I'll take care of
everything. You used to be pretty and so did I but
when life gets difficult you lose your looks. Feel my
hands, they're shaking, it's all the ice they put down
my back, it hurts so much, but they say it's to take
away the pain. What pain? I ask them (*LINDA walks
away, JENINE grabs her.*) I hear a dog barking in the
street and it's the same old story, I know who it is,
it's the wolves, they've got her by the scruff of the
neck, they took her away, they got jealous, outraged
as these people so often are. I can hear them shouting
out there, calling my name but I'm not going to go
out to them, I can say I thought it was voices in my
head. They think I really do hear voices but that's just
the way the wind tunes in like with a radio. I had a
radio down by the rushes by the bridge, a stick like a
divining rod, they'd given her to some Jews and they'd
just left her, I had to look after her all by myself.
There's something not quite right there isn't there?
They put you into care and then they try to make
you work for them. I said listen, if I want to I can take
her to my mother so don't stand over me checking if
I know what I'm doing because I do know, I know and
I've done it all before. They thought she was my first
because I look so young, they always said what a
beautiful complexion I had... I let them take her in the
end, well I just couldn't be bothered, they wanted me
to carry the shit around in a bag, I'm not doing that

I said, how would you like the smell all the time? It's lovely, it's like sour milk they said. How would they bloody know? They're all as dry as parchment, no-one would be able to stick anything up there and get it down again so I know that for certain. If I get £5 now I'll go to Kensington, I need make-up, have you got any? No, you don't need it. No we all could do with it, why not? Come on, let's go out and buy some together. Why do you look so sad? Let me take care of you. Do you know what Mickey said to me, he said you see that girl in there?, she's like a whirlwind in my heart, and when I look at her she's like a bottle opener in my eye

LINDA: Did you notice Mickey has come back?

JENINE: Yes I noticed him by the door

LINDA: You didn't say anything about it

JENINE: I'd rather be here with you

LINDA: Jenine, I'm sorry (*They embrace.*) Thanks for coming round

JENINE: Shall I go?

LINDA: I don't know, stay

JENINE: You can't think of anything else but him

LINDA: Who Jenine?

JENINE: Mickey, Mickey's come back

MICKEY staggers out blindly onto the step.

* * *

Night outside the house, then inside.

MICKEY arrives outside in the dark, the shadow of an old man goes past, he is beating his dog.

MICKEY: Bloody old pooch, hit the bleeder

The shadow stops beating his dog, walks away getting smaller and smaller.

Ah I can see!

Looks about him.

No I can't. Where is everything? Shsh. Quiet, evening Constable, yes (*Smiles.*) all the girls in their summer dresses I see. Oh yes? Got yourself a cosy little number then, you pop across the road for a quick one? Mmm she is a lovely girl yes, I know I was just saying how her well-known hospitality was eating up my... ability to concentrate

No I can't see a thing

A late bird sings in a tree.

Oh a bird singing in a tree

Where's he gone? (*He staggers forward blindly and is inside the room.*)

What's this? A sofa? Suddenly I'm indoors

Whose leg? What kind of a welcome do you call this? A leg outstretched in the dark. I'm going now, clean up in here a bit will you.

I've heard all the streets, the way they behave, and St. Peters street, I can't be bothered shouting at them

Is it dark in here or what? Where's Linda, what've you been saying to her?

No-one understands me that's my trouble

I remember one time Linda and I were trying to get some peace and this geezer comes jumping through the window shooting his mouth off saying he's going to shoot me, I've got a room full of crossbows he says I'll go and fetch one, this blinking neighbourhood

A large motorbike goes past, it's headlight shines into the room.

(*Watches the light as it fills the room.*) Oh look, a sandy beach. (*Searches his pockets.*) Where is everything?

JENINE is in the room sitting on a chair in the corner.

Listen have you stolen my cigarettes?

JENINE: (*Does not reply.*)

MICKEY: Oh. Have you got a cigarette or what?

I mean I just ask you a question and you – would you run over to the garage and get some?

JENINE: Don't hurt me

MICKEY: What are you trying to pull here? I'm ill actually, I'm going to have a lie down

JENINE: (*Says nothing.*)

MICKEY: What? Who? Yes she's here somewhere, have a look, I'm recently blind. Even my hearing is dodgy. Music in one ear my own voice in the other. You're in my way I'd like to stumble about in peace. Is who here?

JENINE: (*Mumbles a name.*)

MICKEY: No but her mum will be here soon, our children too, her father, all her relations, we're planning a party, a family do, party games, old people the whole lot

JENINE: (*Cries out suddenly.*) Alright Mickey

MICKEY sits down on the floor.

JENINE walks out of the room.

MR STEVENSON: You look ill

MICKEY: I am. I am ill

Pause.

MR STEVENSON: Mickey, Mickey, please lend me your shoulder, I'm sorry if, just now I... but now I see in you myself when I was a young man...

MICKEY: (*Laughs.*)

MR STEVENSON: I'm being friendly to you... You can sleep here if you like, have the pick of anything that's going. You don't even have to help around the house

MICKEY: Thanks a lot

MR STEVENSON: (*Grips his arm.*) You'll wish you could have found it in your heart to... Just a little sympathy you know... goes a long way

MICKEY: Where's Linda?

MR STEVENSON: Not here at least. Tell me... You have two women...

MICKEY: I need a third...

MR STEVENSON: Can't help you there, this isn't a brothel

MICKEY: No

MR STEVENSON: No, this is my home

MICKEY: A doss house

MR STEVENSON: If you want to bring some furniture you are welcome. A few sticks would be more than welcome, yes. Come, sit on the bed...

MICKEY: Stop touching me

MR STEVENSON: I could help you make a lot of money, more than I have. I don't begrudge it you, a young man should be free and have a full heart and full pockets, you see?

MICKEY: I see

MR STEVENSON: Oo oo I have a pain here in my arm

MICKEY: Oh

MR STEVENSON: What do you think it is?

MICKEY: Heart attack

MR STEVENSON: Yes, yes!

MICKEY: It wouldn't be the first

MR STEVENSON: What are you talking about, I've had a life of them, don't talk to me my boy about heart attacks

MICKEY: Have you seen my children?

MR STEVENSON: Linda has them. They tire her out. Her face is worn, her tits are sagging. Have you come to save her perhaps?

MICKEY: Do me a favour!

MR STEVENSON: Don't stand there by the window looking out, you clutter my view

MICKEY goes to the door.

What shall I tell her?

Linda. Shall I tell her you're gone out? Will be back after the dark, in the morning, if Linda asks?

MICKEY: I don't care what you tell her

MR STEVENSON: Did she go out with friends?

MICKEY: Eh?

MR STEVENSON: That leaves you free for the other one

MICKEY: I know. That's why I've got her lined up

MR STEVENSON: Have you?

MICKEY: What?

MR STEVENSON: Got her fixed up

MICKEY: Yes, got her fixed up

MR STEVENSON: For tonight, just like that?

MICKEY: Yes. Want to come?

MR STEVENSON: Come? Me?

MICKEY: Yes

MR STEVENSON: What... Why yes, yes, I'd come. Where are we going?

MICKEY: Nowhere

MR STEVENSON: Nowhere? Oh but who'll open the door to Linda?

MICKEY: She has a key

MR STEVENSON: But who'll make up her bed?

MICKEY: What? She's got a bed?

MR STEVENSON: The kids then, who'll see to them?

MICKEY: Fuck the kids

MR STEVENSON: Alright then

MICKEY: Yeah, let her deal with that

MR STEVENSON: Who?

MICKEY: Linda

MR STEVENSON: Yeah, let Linda deal with it

*   *   *

MICKEY and LINDA walking arm in arm by the edge of a lake.

MICKEY: This must be the 500th time we've done this

LINDA: Yes

MICKEY: ... It always ends up the same way though doesn't it?

LINDA: ...

MICKEY: ... Still never mind. You and me, lovers from prehistoric times until yesterday... no I mean forever and ever

Pause.

What's the matter? Stomach ache?

LINDA: Yes

MICKEY: Earache?

LINDA: (*Sighs, rubs her hand on her stomach.*) I feel...

MICKEY: You feel...? What?

LINDA: I feel...

MICKEY: There's always something bloody wrong

LINDA: I can't help it

MICKEY: I know. (*Strokes her head.*) Never mind, poor little baby, nothing's quite right is it?

LINDA: (*Pained expression searching inside for the seat of the pain.*) I... just

MICKEY: Yes

LINDA: I feel...

MICKEY: Oh I know. Poor thing

LINDA: (*Looks at him, drops her eyes to the ground to hide her anger.*)

MICKEY: So anyway I said to this geezer I can see you like living down the road from her, alright mate, you may think you're doing her a favour but you ain't 'cause she don't need no favours doing, she's all bloody favours all day long. Oh. Aren't you listening?

LINDA: Yes

MICKEY: Don't just let me ramble on on my own

LINDA: I...

MICKEY: (*Stops her.*) I mean don't...

LINDA: I...

MICKEY: (*Stops her.*) I mean what kind of a life is this...

LINDA: I...

MICKEY: (*Stops her.*) Really? For me?

LINDA: Mickey I...

MICKEY: Look at that water, what a stinking hole

LINDA: (*Looks without seeing, blinded by her thoughts.*)

MICKEY: Don't just pretend to look. Rags everywhere, in the reeds, look rags, rag dolls, little things wrapped in rags, aren't you interested? Look there's a little rag doll in the water floating along, look at it, don't just, a real bloody... lying there, someone must have put it there, it didn't bloody arrive by itself

LINDA: Yes

MICKEY: Don't just say yes, look at it

LINDA: (*Looks.*)

MICKEY: No, look because you want to see it. It's not every day you see a real rag doll

LINDA: Mmm

MICKEY: Go on pick it up, alright I'll pick it up. (*Picks it up, hands it to her.*) There, there, look after it or something...

LINDA: (*Holds it absently.*)

MICKEY: (*Snatches it from her.*) If you can't forget about
   yourself just for one moment, then I'll... No I won't,
   I don't care about bleeding rag dolls (*Throws it in the water.
   Stares after it.*)

LINDA: (*Pretends to stare after it too but she doesn't see it because she
   is thinking.*)

MICKEY: I said I don't care about rag dolls

LINDA: (*Stares at him passively.*)

MICKEY: You bloody evil bitch

LINDA: (*Stares.*)

MICKEY: Aren't you happy out here? I thought we'd go for
   a walk together...

LINDA: Shall I go and change?

MICKEY: Do what you like

LINDA: Shall I put my hair in a ponytail?

MICKEY: Yes do that

LINDA: I'm sorry Mickey, it's when I feel you don't
   appreciate me

   *They arrive at where JENINE is crouching by the shallows dipping
   something into the water.*

MICKEY: What are you doing?

JENINE: I'm trying to wash my heart. (*She gets up, her peace
   disturbed, drops the heart into the water.*) Why haven't you
   been to see me? You seem to be cooling off, that's never
   happened before. I suppose you're tired of it all. I am.
   Linda is. You must be

   Pause. She smiles, then changes.

   Oh Mickey, it's so painful, it's worse than ever, look what
   it's done to me... I'm Linda's slave now aren't I Linda?

LINDA: She does me little favours

JENINE: In exchange for cigarettes

LINDA: Yes we're friends again

JENINE: She's the model for my phantom pregnancies, look. (*She smoothes her clothes over the curve of her belly.*)

LINDA: How that little bulge used to scare me

JENINE: Yes, now it's Linda that scares me

LINDA: – and that's the way it should be

JENINE: Isn't it Mickey?

MICKEY: (*Does not reply.*)

JENINE: Don't worry. I'm sure there's fun and games left in the future. You don't need to take this seriously it's not the end of anything. I'm sure we'll manage something no one else has ever managed

LINDA: Shall we invite Jenine to dinner Mickey?

JENINE: I can come and eat the crumbs from your table

LINDA: Yes and we'll get to know each other all over again

JENINE: I hope I can behave as well as I've behaved just now

LINDA: She's been alright hasn't she Mickey?

JENINE: So has Mickey

LINDA: Mickey? Oh no, he's alright

MICKEY turns and walks away.

JENINE: (*Calls after him.*) I'll try not to be a baby

She returns to the waters edge.

* * *

A table set. MR STEVENSON, JENINE and MICKEY sit already, LINDA comes out down the steps.

LINDA: There, the children are asleep in their little beds

MR STEVENSON: Good we can begin. (*Tucks napkin.*) What are we celebrating?

LINDA: Mickey's come home

JENINE: Mickey's birthday

MR STEVENSON: (*To LINDA.*) Come on, come on. Here sit on my knee pet

MICKEY: Get your hands off her

JENINE: Mickey

MICKEY: Yes my flaxen-haired angel?

MR STEVENSON: How are we all feeling?

LINDA: Fine

JENINE: ... Please sit next to me

Pause.

MICKEY: ... Of course

MR STEVENSON: Linda would you feed me...?

LINDA: Oh...

MR STEVENSON: Only the difficult bits...

MICKEY: I can hear the kids crying

MR STEVENSON: No you can't

MICKEY: Yes I can

MR STEVENSON: You're just making it up. You go if it's that important

MICKEY: I didn't say it's important, I said I can hear them. Shall *I* feed you?

MR STEVENSON: No I want her to do it, my daughter

MICKEY: Shall I feed you Jenine

JENINE: No, I don't...

MR STEVENSON: Yes you feed her

LINDA: I think I heard them

MICKEY: Did you?

JENINE: Where are *my* babies?

Pause.

MICKEY: If you heard them go and see

JENINE: Mickey...

LINDA: Food anyone?

MR STEVENSON: How lovely she serves. You look so well my dear. (*LINDA serves MR STEVENSON.*) Thank you Linda, that's very nice

LINDA: Jenine?

JENINE: No, I'm not hungry

MR STEVENSON: Linda's got lovely fat arms now...

LINDA sits, they eat, pause.

Linda you're not concentrating, your soup is running down your front

She carries on eating.

Linda!

JENINE: I'll just have a banana.

MICKEY: What are you eating a banana for?

JENINE: Why not?

MR STEVENSON: Linda, by the way where's the –

MICKEY: Wine

MR STEVENSON: The wine, yes where's the wine?

LINDA: There's none left, I drank it

MR STEVENSON: You drank it?

JENINE: Get me some

LINDA: There isn't any, Jenine

JENINE: It is your babies crying I can hear

MICKEY: Yes I can too

LINDA: Let them cry

MR STEVENSON: Poor little darlings, need a cry I should think

LINDA: Bleeders

JENINE: I just want to have a –

LINDA: A what?

JENINE: A look

LINDA: Go on then

JENINE: Is there any wine?

MICKEY: She's drunk it all

LINDA: Yes and now I feel sleepy

JENINE: I'll take a look then. (*Doesn't move.*)

MR STEVENSON: Linda, you're not feeding me

LINDA: I need a sleep, a few minutes should do it

LINDA climbs onto the table and lies down.

MR STEVENSON: How can you display yourself like this

MICKEY keeps on eating.

MR STEVENSON: Didn't I bring you up to be shy?

LINDA: (*Falling asleep.*) Yes...

MR STEVENSON: Your dress has ridden up over your thighs. (*He catches sight of MICKEY.*) Mickey! You have had more than your fair share of strawberries

MICKEY: Have I?

MR STEVENSON: Yes

MICKEY: I took exactly the same as Linda. I knew you'd be watching me

MR STEVENSON: Linda can take as many as she likes

JENINE: Mickey I brought you a potted plant

MICKEY: Thank you

JENINE: It's a geranium. Put it in the window to show that love's poison never dies

MR STEVENSON: Didn't you use to carry around a neat little black handbag?

JENINE: I dropped it..

MR STEVENSON: ... and go everywhere in a taxi?

JENINE: Yes

MR STEVENSON: And now you are cadging cigarettes I hear

JENINE: So many wolves around my breaking heart... Still at least *you* are happy Mickey. I remember when you would pretend to be blind, you were so coarse and rude, now all your aggression has faded, isn't that nice?

MICKEY: (*Stands.*) Would you like to walk along the beach with me?

JENINE: I'm married now

MICKEY: Are you? (*Sits.*)

JENINE: You don't mind?

MICKEY: Children?

JENINE: There's one in my womb at this very moment

MICKEY: Ah

JENINE: The size of a pea...

MICKEY: It's not mine? Is it?

JENINE: It couldn't be

MICKEY: Of course not

   Pause.

   Are you sure you have a child inside you the size of a pea?

JENINE: Not one hundred percent

MICKEY: There is some uncertainty?

MR STEVENSON: Stop this at once!

JENINE: Be quiet Mr Stevenson, you'll wake Linda

MR STEVENSON: She ought to be awake... and cover herself up

JENINE: She's happy the way she is

MR STEVENSON: She's such a whore

MICKEY: Rubbish

JENINE: It makes her feel happy and free Mr Stevenson to have something people want. It's an expression of... her inner light...

MR STEVENSON: Come, come

JENINE: Of the soul that burns behind her shifty eyes, the dullest, most lifeless eyes...

MR STEVENSON: (*Has stopped listening, shakes LINDA to wake her.*) Linda, Linda!

JENINE: ... apart from your own... and if you set her free she'll burst into flames like a –

MICKEY: (*Stroking LINDA's head.*) ... Piece of toast

JENINE: ... and live... and love

MR STEVENSON: I don't wish to hear

JENINE: ... with an open heart

MR STEVENSON: It's obscene. Don't you think I know my own daughter?

JENINE: Linda's tired because she is pregnant

MICKEY: Yes

MR STEVENSON: Ah no, sadly the little pink patches in her knickers tell us otherwise, yes. (*Strokes LINDA's head.*)

JENINE: No baby? But there has to be! I've taught myself to love it, it has cost me so much!

MR STEVENSON: Oh, there is a little baby the size of a pea, but it's not as big as it should be... and the little love has pains too... I feel them as well of course...

JENINE: There is a baby...

MR STEVENSON: But it's dead, dead but clinging on
nevertheless

JENINE: No! please!

MR STEVENSON: We've arranged to have it scraped out
haven't we lovey?

MICKEY: Can I be there. I am the father. I hope

MR STEVENSON: It's not a spectator sport my boy...
They use a kind of hoover I believe...

MICKEY: Oh well...

JENINE: (*Cries.*) But I wanted her to have this baby

Pause. JENINE sobs bitterly.

MR STEVENSON: Well who's going to do the washing up?

MICKEY: Linda............ Lazy tart

MR STEVENSON: Why are you crying? is it sympathy for
my daughter?

JENINE: (*Crying.*) No, no... Yes

MR STEVENSON: It's not the end of the world. They'll
have many more

MICKEY eats the leftovers and drains the last glass of squash.

JENINE: Yes

MR STEVENSON: I'll buy them a car one day, I think,
make them like a real family, you know

JENINE: Yes

MR STEVENSON: ... Linda has started dressing smartly,
have you noticed?

JENINE: Yes I have noticed

MR STEVENSON: (*He runs his hand along the sleeping LINDA.*) See her skirt, and these shoes? She's a lovely girl isn't she?

JENINE: (*Dries her eyes, stands up, gathers herself.*) Actually, I'm tired of hearing that. I think she's plain

MR STEVENSON: Her very plainness seems to attract. Look at Mickey... He's like a dog chasing after a b –

JENINE: No... She's very average

MR STEVENSON: ... chasing after a bitch on heat... You must have noticed

JENINE: I don't think about it...

MR STEVENSON: Sit down. Aren't you well?

JENINE sits down. MICKEY drinks a flagon of water. MR STEVENSON looks at him with irritation.

JENINE: I think...

MR STEVENSON: You think?

JENINE: I think... Mickey is wasted on her. He's fooling himself if he thinks –

MR STEVENSON: If he thinks...?

JENINE: ... he'll get anything out of her

MR STEVENSON thinks. Pause.

MR STEVENSON: Get what out of her?

MICKEY consumes some grapes.

JENINE: I think he feels invisible

MR STEVENSON: (*To MICKEY.*) Could you pass me a grape

MICKEY: None left

JENINE: Do you know what I mean?

MR STEVENSON: What? (*He has forgotten she is there.*)

JENINE: About Mickey, you see I don't think he's very happy, in fact he can never he –

MR STEVENSON: (*To MICKEY.*) What?

JENINE: Not with her

MR STEVENSON: Not one?

MICKEY: No

MR STEVENSON: Sponger

JENINE: I admit, I'm not any better for him myself now

MR STEVENSON: I'll throw you out of this house one day

JENINE: ... But that's because I'm paralysed by the pain of my broken heart

MR STEVENSON: You have devoured my fruit my boy

JENINE: But if got the chance I'd be perfect

MR STEVENSON: You've spoiled my garden with your motorcycle

MICKEY bites into an apple. LINDA snores.

You've ploughed furrows in my lawn

JENINE: I'd be perfect! (*Stands up and sweeps the crockery off the table.*)

Short pause. MR STEVENSON looks at her.

(*More calmly.*) Mickey is frightened to change anything for the better, you see

MR STEVENSON: I think I'll awaken Linda. (*He slides his hand across the table to her foot. MICKEY snatches up*

MR STEVENSON's walking stick and brings it down with a crack upon MR STEVENSON's hand.)

Oh my hand, my hand, he's broken my hand!

Blood streams from his hand.

Look all my fingers are twisted. You madman

MICKEY stands before JENINE.

JENINE: Is that the best you can do?

MR STEVENSON: How dare you intrude upon my person. (*He stands up.*) My stick is snapped in half, how will I walk?

He staggers from the table.

He staggers back again.

I shall wake her, I shall wake her, Linda, wake up darling, look at what has happened

LINDA wakes up with a start, her face contorted momentarily by imbecility which passes as she becomes fully awake two seconds later.

LINDA: What?

MR STEVENSON: Look at Daddy's hand

LINDA: Oh what's happened?

MR STEVENSON: Come and help me inside my dear, I'm in shock

LINDA sits up on the table. MR STEVENSON helps her as she slides sleepily to the ground, he catches her in his arms and pulls down the dress which has rumpled up in the process.

MR STEVENSON: We'll go and have a little sleep on the mattress.

LINDA catches sight of MICKEY and JENINE standing five feet apart staring into each others eyes.

LINDA: Wait, what are they doing?

JENINE: It's alright Linda I was just saying goodbye

MR STEVENSON: Do help me Linda, I'm bleeding, look

LINDA: You're always saying goodbye

MR STEVENSON: (*Hobbles up to MICKEY.*) You're always saying goodbye. (*He waves his bloody hand in his face.*)

LINDA: I can't ever get any peace

MR STEVENSON: (*To MICKEY.*) Let me have some peace

Pause.

Come on my baby, daddy's depressed, his knuckles are in shatters, we'll bathe them

LINDA turns to go with him casting a glance of hatred at him as she does so, which passes without her noticing.

They go inside together.

MICKEY stands where he is without moving, JENINE has the air of one about to leave.

JENINE: Mickey, that's Linda's old jumper isn't it?

MICKEY: Yes

JENINE: (*With tears and anger.*) Take it off

MICKEY pulls off the jumper he is wearing and then JENINE walks away.

MICKEY sits at the table and searches idly for more leftovers.

The End.

THE TERRIBLE VOICE OF SATAN

THE TERRIBLE VOICE OF SATAN was first performed at The Royal Court Theatre Upstairs in July 1993. It was directed by James MacDonald, with the following cast:

Simon Carter

Katrin Cartlidge

Denys Hawthorne

Leda Hodgson

Mairead McKinley

Dan Mullane

Sean Murray

Michael O'Connor

Elizabeth Critchfield

Jack Rickson

Bille Temple

Designer: Bunny Christie

A man at a urinal.

MAN: This is the story of Tom Doheny, a figure in popular lore, some fools say he was the devil, some say just a plain honest Irish man. Some say he was two fellas, some three, others that the trinity was divisible, or that he was a boatload of adventurers, others that Tom Doheny was the name of the boat itself, but then in that case who was it came on the boat, and where did they put ashore and inevitably what were their names and what the name of their god? This last is answered, albeit partially, by the old saying: if you want to know a people's god, look at their devil. Your lordships I give you Tom Doheny, hero, heroine, vessel of all our hopes, traitor, thief, braggart

Lights out.

Hey! Ah my shoes!

* * *

TOM DOHENY, a man with enormous boots, wheels a wheelbarrow. Inside it is a skinny white-haired old woman, his mother. Out in front, a tired old man in a filthy grey suit is walking as if leading the party, but though he manipulates his cane boldly he is lost.

MA: Get some speed up Tom, we'll be perished by the cold

TOM: Why don't you give us a song as we go

MA: I will not. I have sung my throat to ribbons over the Christmas festivities, I'm voiceless

TOM: A great quality in a mother

MA: Never you mind your qualities get some elbow into it. Oh why did we have to come on the boat, why didn't we fly over like decent people?

DA: The boat's fine

MA: Gee you're earthbound if ever a man was. Don't be earthbound like your father son

DA: You trample me into the mud with every word and then you expect me to rise like a phoenix from the pile of insults you heap on top of me. I'd just as soon die now and be done with it. Stop off now at this cemetery on the left son and save yourself the trouble later on

MA: Go on but who'll dig your grave for you? I can't see you doing it. No, I guess you're stuck in the land of the living, too bone idle to die

DA: Bone idle is it? There's more calluses on these hands than on your face even

A beautiful woman walks past, effortlessly overtaking the wheelbarrow and striding off ahead.

MA: What was that?

TOM: My future wife

MA: Ha listen to him. Good luck to you son

TOM: Wait there (*He clomps off in haste hindered by his giant shoes.*)

MA: Your son's gone to make a fool of himself, running after that mare with great long legs on her and the devil's own petticoat or what was she wearing?

DA: What do I care? This is all a dream. I'm still at home with the piggies

Enter a PRIEST in a long black cassock.

PRIEST: No, wrong. You're in God's house.

MA: Ah you frightened me father! But this is the edge of a turnip field, a beach beside the sea

PRIEST: You are a disgrace to the Irish race! Don't you realise this is a cathedral? You are inside one of the biggest churches in the world

DA: Jeez, they make 'em big here

PRIEST: That's right fella, you'd better get used to it.
Quick now, down on your knees and beg forgiveness
before anyone sees you, come on, come on

He forces them to kneel in the mud.

The wind begins to howl.

Don't you know the devil stalks these cliffs looking for
souls such as yours. He's around here now. Pray for
God's sake!

The old couple clasp their hands together in prayer and start mumbling.

Thunder and lightning.

He'll make monsters of us all, he'll creep up on you and
climb up on your shoulder and be there whispering and
whispering until you can't bear it. Because do you know
what he does, do you know what Satan does?

MA *and* DA: (*In terror.*) No father, what does he do?

PRIEST: He speaks the truth!

Thunder and lightning.

MA *and* DA: Argh! (*They cower in horror at these words.*)

PRIEST: Pray! Go on in Christ's name pray!

DA: Will you pray with us father?

PRIEST: Don't be ridiculous man! I've got to keep the look out.

He tugs at his hair in despair as they fall to praying.

TOM comes back making them all jump.

PRIEST: This is him! Get behind me Satan!

TOM: What's going on?

DA: The good father has advised we should pray son, where
have you been?

TOM: Aah, I've been and picked these seven wild flowers with that young lady. And now I will sleep with them under my pillow and with any luck I'll dream of the one I am to marry. She'll do the same with the seven she picked – what a great girl – Goodnight

He takes off one of his enormous boots and places the seven flowers under it and rests his head upon it as a pillow.

PRIEST: (*Crosses himself.*) Good night good people, God bless and protect you, snuff the candles on your way out

*   *   *

TOM sleeps. A dark shape appears at his feet dancing in the darkness, occasionally struck by lightning as it does so.

MAGIC BIRD: Ah Tom, Tom Doheny, so you're here after all at last. Haven't I been waiting for you?

TOM: Who are you?

MAGIC BIRD: I am the Magic Bird that dances at your feet, I'm the girl you are to marry, I'm your tombstone too, they call it a headstone but what do they know? The stone is always at your feet boy. Now tell me, what will you do here?

TOM: Don't ask me, I'm here on account of my ambitious mother

MAGIC BIRD: Parents. You don't need them now! Send them off to sea!

TOM: No-one needs them now poor loves, thinking of them brings a lump to my throat

MAGIC BIRD: A lump? Hope it's not cancer. I hear it can be painful

Grabs his knee boisterously.

TOM: Argh! What's that?

MAGIC BIRD: That's the old knee-grab; a playful tool to see if you're awake. Come on now take me to Holy Joe's I want to pray

TOM: We're already there sir

MAGIC BIRD: Alright then, on your knees. Now what will you ask His Reverence for? A new job or a new life altogether? Come on make your mind up, I haven't got all day.

TOM: This must be a dream

MAGIC BIRD: If you don't like it you can leave, I'm not here to dance favour on you laddoe

TOM: Stop jumping about, sit still!

MAGIC BIRD: I can't, I have to keep moving or I'll be struck by lightning. It's the curse His Lordship put on me when I told him what I thought of him

TOM: Did you? Did you do that?

MAGIC BIRD: Of course I did, what do you take me for?

TOM: That's what I'd like to be like, bold and frightening

MAGIC BIRD: You already are, I'd heard of you

TOM: Had you?

MAGIC BIRD: (*Suddenly aggressive.*) Can't find anyone to blame!? Well then, you'll have to wind your neck in!

TOM: What?

*   *   *

TOM catches up with the PRIEST.

Father, Father, wait!

PRIEST: So it's you

TOM: I'm not bad father, I swear to you

PRIEST: I know. I know it. Forgive me

TOM: I'm just a simple working man

PRIEST: The problem is my boy that I've gone mad.
I have delusions. I'd seek a cure apart from the fact
that I rather like them

TOM: Actually I came to ask you a favour

PRIEST: Good lad. I could tell by your blackened teeth
you were a man to be trusted. What can I do for you?

TOM: Marry me to that long-legged girl I was with tonight

PRIEST: If you can find her, I'll do it for you. Though
strictly I'm enjoying an early retirement on account of
my doctrinal hesitations

TOM: Can't those be overcome, with study father?

PRIEST: Isn't that precisely what my Lord Bishop said to
me yesterday. I have a little grog under my cot if you
care to follow me home. You could perhaps help me out
of my anathema

They set off.

Oh, what about your aged parents?

TOM: I left them parked in the swamp, they seemed happy
enough with it

PRIEST: Bless them

*   *   *

*TOM DOHENY's head appears from a hole at ground level.
Along comes a pair of boots and a pair of ladies shoes.*

NELLIE: What's that?

MAN: A navvy's head. Otherwise known as the devil's football

The head starts digging.

NELLIE: What are you doing?

TOM: Digging missus

NELLIE: He's digging. He's ever so strong. What muscles!

A VOICE SOME WAY OFF: Come up out of that hole and help us Tom Doheny

The head smiles to itself.

MAN: You bloody navvy, what do you have to keep digging holes for? Don't you know people fall into them and hurt themselves! For Christ's sake soon the whole world will be a paddy's hole.

TOM: I know what you mean and all health to your worship. I'd stop right now if it weren't for one thing

NELLIE: What's that?

TOM: My poor dead mummy and daddy

A pair of black brogues under a cassock appears alongside the boots and shoes.

PRIEST: Nonsense Tom, they're right as rain, sure there's nothing the matter with them at all. Hardly what you'd call dead at any rate

TOM: Alright so. It's for my friend the priest. It's for his sake alone that I am digging

PRIEST: It's true. It's all on account of me

NELLIE: I'm in love, I'm in love with the Navvy's head. What a wonderful man!

TOM: Actually as it happens I'm not just a labouring man, I've many talents to benefit the world. I'm a doctor and, and a poet –

NELLIE: What poems have you written?

TOM: None to date. Travelling is my first love

NELLIE: Where have you been?

TOM: Across the Irish Sea. Twice

NELLIE: Twice? But you're in England. What was your original point of departure?

TOM: Well dammit that's peculiar

NELLIE: Alright help him up, he's a genius. We'll set him on the road to riches

PRIEST: Really no, I'd leave him there

NELLIE: No I can't. His little head looks so sorrowful at shoe level

TOM: I like the idea of a new job Dan, it'd be an awful boost. And think of all the fun we'd have if I got rich

PRIEST: I'll not be having fun with you Tom Doheny!

TOM: The reverend father is embarrassed on account of all the evenings he and I passed the jar to and fro between us, the old tongue loosens, he's said some things I suppose he'd rather I didn't repeat

PRIEST: In the name of God Tom I'm a man like any other

TOM: I'm not holding it against you Dan

PRIEST: He's a terrible one for the ladies as well, you can't trust him

NELLIE: Give us your hands Tom. Come on father help me

They all reach down and pull. They tumble into the hole, boots, shoes and brogues.

Lights up. A girl on a bicycle, dressed in white rides past.

Lights down.

Bicycle and rider clatter down into the hole in the dark.

*   *   *

TOM DOHENY and an elderly FRIEND.

TOM: So anyway I went into the hospital in an old white coat and started off with a few experiments of my own and what do you know? I'd discovered 17 real important cures

FRIEND: There's the true luck of the Irish for you

TOM: It all came from nowhere. My head was buzzing with inventions and marvels of all kinds. I pick up a pen and a beautiful poem appears. I whistle in the bathtub and I end up constructing cherubic melodies

FRIEND: Here's my hand on that. I always said you were a great lad, a real success. Good boy! Good lad!

TOM: But here's the real crux

FRIEND: What? What is it?

TOM: I discovered it was all worthless

FRIEND: What? Worthless? A mistake surely

TOM: Dross

FRIEND: All your discoveries, your love songs?

TOM: All of it

FRIEND: The injections for little babies?

TOM: Nothing at all. Worse than nothing

FRIEND: I'm sorry to hear that. Whatever brought you to this conclusion?

TOM: I have found their replacement, an inheritor

FRIEND: A replacement? What can it be?

TOM: I have discovered it

FRIEND: What kind of thing is it?

TOM: It is, the Magic Bird

FRIEND: A bird?

TOM: The cure of all ills upon us currently

FRIEND: What was it you called this thing?

TOM: The Magic Bird

*   *   *

The two lovers on a sandy beach together.

TOM: ... and then there's my inheritance from my parents
(*Crosses himself.*) God preserve them from all harm

NELLIE: Are they rich? They appeared destitute

TOM: They are modest people. Beneath their indigent
exteriors are hidden great stores of physical and spiritual
wealth. They are like two turtle doves whispering to each
other all day

NELLIE: (*She secretly cuts her foot with a broken glass.*) That must
be a great inspiration to you

TOM: It is yes. Don't you worry about me Captain because
I'm a great believer in romance

NELLIE: Oh so am I, so am I!

TOM: We'll be great together

NELLIE: Oh Tom...

TOM: Yes darlin'?

NELLIE: I've hurt my foot

*   *   *

TOM DOHENY and his MATES, labourers.

TOM: Yes boys I think I'll settle down

MATES: No, No!

TOM: Yes lads the time has come to lay down my fiddle, take off my boots and drain the last jar. After all I've a good woman waiting for me

LIAM: But many others besides, don't forget them, bless their poor wayward hearts, the wild flowers of the wayside, condemned to blow forever, plagued by flies and the tinkers snout

TOM: Enough boys. I can't bear any more! Alright I'll come out one more time with ye. We'll drink a toast: To England that has made itself my home and raised me to great heights of fame

RORY: But don't forget–

TOM: – Ireland, the wild flower of the wayside

FINN: Where'll we go?

TOM: Up to Camden, then beyond to Archway and beyant...

LIAM: What'll we do there?

TOM: We'll strip down to our woollies and dance with the plump girls of the North

RORY: And the lean colleens of the South

LIAM: Swing from infernal Archway Tower – and balance walk the rails of Suicide Bridge

TOM *and* ALL: Off we go!

They go.

TOM stays behind, the girl on the bike cycles round him. He smiles at her. She stops alongside him. The moon appears, switches on like a lamp. A nightingale sings a sudden song.

*   *   *

TOM and his MATES, at the dog-end of the evening, the dawn.

LIAM: Hello there Tom

TOM: Lads!

RORY: What became of you?

TOM: Oh! One of them wild flowers of the wayside turned up and I was indisposed to join you on your hedgerow rambles

LIAM: He's laughing at us is he?

FINN: Is he? Are you laughing at us Tom?

LIAM: Is that it Hah?

RORY: You've some strange English habits Tom

TOM: Is that it? Well then lads, yes I am laughing at you

LIAM: Another wise crack and you'll be laughing with a cracked lip

TOM: But lads I had a great adventure. Surely you don't think I should pass up on that to hold hands with you lot?

RORY: He's too good for us

FINN: You could have introduced us

LIAM: No, we're as common as dirt

RORY: Didn't she have any friends?

TOM: Fortunately not if my so-called friends are anything
     to go by

RORY: You'll get along fine Tom

FINN: Yes, you'll be a great scholar

LIAM: I reckon he'll end up an Englishman so he will

RORY: Only don't count on our support when you're
      running for President of America

TOM: Thanks lads for this

FINN: You'd best go back to your film producers and your
      cardinals now Doheny

TOM: I will, thanks

RORY: Go back to your English virgins, if you can find them

FINN: Yeah and all your literate friends

LIAM: All the nobs, go on back to them and see if they're
      the gullible crowd you took us for

TOM: Oh I'm sure they are lads don't worry

*   *   *

TOM DOHENY wheels his wife along in a wheelbarrow.

NELLIE: I suppose I must be a great disappointment to you

TOM: Not at all

NELLIE: I bet you're thinking: "I wouldn't have married
        her if I'd known I would end up wheeling her about, it's
        not a nursemaid I wanted to be"

TOM: You're quite wrong. I hadn't really noticed

NELLIE: I catch you looking at me. Don't you think
        I know I'm holding you back. You could be out
        somewhere with a healthy lass having a world of fun

TOM: We have fun sometimes the two of us

NELLIE: You don't call this fun do you?

TOM: Well it might be if you'd only stop moaning

NELLIE: Always that word of criticism

TOM: I only said–

NELLIE: You criticise until there is nothing left of a person. You take away even their right to be wrong. In fact if it weren't for your constant scrutiny I wouldn't perhaps be like this. Have you thought of that?

TOM: No I've never thought of that

NELLIE: I remember the day, it was a week ago now, our wedding day, that you first complained about my limp

TOM: I wasn't complaining on my behalf

NELLIE: Don't tell me you were proud to have your new wife staggering as if three parts drunk. I've seen you watching those girls go past with their big strides

TOM: Why don't you walk then?

NELLIE: I've lost all confidence. Every time I fell over I felt your eyes burning into me

TOM: Then for God's sake get up and walk and I'll turn my back. Or walk off so I won't find you

NELLIE: I can't! Look! (*She throws herself out from the wheelbarrow.*)

TOM: You didn't even try

NELLIE: I can't try, that's just it. I tried to try but something stopped me

TOM: Then I don't know what I can do

NELLIE: I'll keep trying to try

TOM: How will I know when you are making that particular effort?

NELLIE: You'll feel a tremor in the barrow. You must have noticed?

TOM: Yes, a slight tremor, rarely

NELLIE: That's the signal

TOM: The tremor serves unaccountably to remind me of the passing of time. It's like a knell. Can't we do without it?

NELLIE: Only if I stop trying. And you want me to try don't you. Otherwise you would feel bound to me like this for ever. Then the absence of a tremor would also be a knell, the difference being that it would be constant. A constant absence of tremor. You choose

TOM: I can't. Everything is a reminder. Death itself is reduced to the role of a reminder

NELLIE: You mean I am worse than a fatal disease?

TOM: Yes you are like a disease that is not fatal and therefore has no end

NELLIE: I'm surprised to find this cantankerous side in you. When I saw you in your hole I thought you would be above small differences. I noticed the way you served your poor parents digging your father's grave at his command regardless of his obstinate good health, a dutiful son I thought. A firm hand on a shovel if one was needed. Instead I find you an egotist. After all, I have my good days when I am up and running, then my legs are like anyone else's, better in fact. (*Hitches up her dress and shows him her gartered thigh.*) If there's company. I don't hear you praising me for that

TOM: I'm always praising you. I praise you so much I nearly believe it myself

NELLIE: What a bitter man, and what a bully

*   *   *

TOM stands wearily. The PRIEST approaches.

PRIEST: I've bad news for you Tom

TOM: Well don't be shy with it nothing could bring me
down now, I'm on the crest of a wave

PRIEST: Your parents have drowned

TOM: Both of them? Jeez, it never rains

PRIEST: Terrible when you consider it was you sent them
on a luxury cruise from the proceeds of your...

TOM: I have returned them to the sea whence they came

*   *   *

A graveyard on top of a hill.

PRIEST: Look at the view there, isn't it marvellous!

TOM: Mercy we are high up, I didn't notice the climb

A funeral cortege arrives alongside them.

PRIEST: Well, Tom, let's get on and bury them shall we?

TOM: They came and whispered into my ear

PRIEST: Who whispered in your ear?

TOM: The laddoes left a sly bottle of whiskey, just left it on
the side there as they went out

PRIEST: There's a good crowd anyway

TOM: I find the bitterness of death only partially alleviated
by the joviality of a funeral

The PRIEST reads from his book in latin.

SEXTON: You know there's nothing in dem boxes

GORMLESS PAL: Nothing at all?

SEXTON: Not a bone. Sure the two of them were lost at sea

GORMLESS PAL: Diabolical luck

TOM's wife NELLIE struggles along, drunk, not in mourning.

NELLIE: Father forgive me I know I shouldn't be here like this but maybe you can help me. I need something, something is missing, there always has been but what is it?

PRIEST: I'm sure I don't know

NELLIE: Oh but I do! Guidance father. I need someone to tell me right from wrong

PRIEST: Well I'm the last person to come to for that

NELLIE: Father you must help me I'm past despair

PRIEST: Not my department girlie, I'm likely more depressed than you are. Now Tom Doheny's more your man...

NELLIE: Tom? Hah ha. He's no help at all. It's Tom Doheny this, Tom Doheny that, everyone has such high regard for his talents but what is he? A navvy. Such rumours spread, he's a doctor, a businessman, a politician, a real solver of problems. Well I'll tell you about Tom Doheny: He has another woman

PRIEST: Is this true Tom?

TOM: I wouldn't say 'have'

PRIEST: What sophistry is that? Have you or haven't you?

NELLIE: He's *had* her is what he means to say

PRIEST: Please Nellie I know Tom wouldn't boast in that vulgar way about what shall we call them, his amorous adventures

TOM: Quite right

NELLIE: I've seen him riding on the back of her bicycle in the moonlight when he ought to have been with me

PRIEST: I take a dim view Tom

TOM: Christ Father, she was a perfect stranger. I was attending to her inner tube

PRIEST: Well, if that's true my son –

NELLIE: What? Astride her panniers? That's a damned unusual position

TOM: The unusual positions are sometimes the best

NELLIE : (*Recoils in horror.*) You see! And this is the man you'd have me take as my moral guide

PRIEST: But what kind of ethical certainties do you require? I think you're setting your demands too high. After all you are only an ordinary woman, it's not as if you are about to scale any peaks of virtue or, I hope, plough any troughs of malcreancy

NELLIE: You're wrong. My inner landscape has to be seen to be believed

PRIEST: Take your wife in hand Tom. Give her what she needs. You must have picked her for this interesting side of her nature

TOM: Yes indeed she looked at me with such penetration I was bewitched

PRIEST: There you are then

TOM: But I had mistaken it. She was in fact gawping in utter confusion. Am I right?

NELLIE: True father. I am not of this world. It's a mystery to me. It's all in a foreign language. They speak to me of many things but my ears are searching only for words of sympathy, I am deaf to all else

PRIEST: Then my son you are a fool and have only yourself to blame

NELLIE: What should I do? (*Turns to TOM.*) Those seven flowers, you have trampled them

TOM: And you?

NELLIE: Should I offer hope? Where shall I go? Away? Alone?

TOM: No, you'd only return

* * *

On a hilltop, a DRY LITTLE MAN in an anorak.

A wild wind blows then fades away.

The wind comes again.

DRY MAN: So, you've come to the point in your life when you'd like some power

TOM: Right! I'm past crucifying age, now I want what's mine

DRY MAN: Then rise up and take it

TOM: But... my energies are beginning to flag

DRY MAN: That's tough luck indeed...

TOM: What wickedness is it forces a young man to spend his best energies kicking his heels and then be called upon to raise the battle cry just when his life is crumbling about his ears

DRY MAN: You'd best put a brave face on it because your difficulties will only grow from now on

TOM: I'm in the grips of a terrible fear, I'm scared of the dark but I can't stand the light, I can't bear company but I can't be alone, I can neither travel nor stay put...

DRY MAN: Try to be a man for God's sake!

TOM: All my energies are spent watching my loved ones suffer and myself suffer at their hands

DRY MAN: I'll give you hope

TOM: I want shelter. I look at you and I see a desert. I don't want it

DRY MAN: Oh I know you're hankering for fruit, soft pears in the sunshine, a peaceful garden and a lake, but what's beckoning there is nothing but death itself. You must deny it and follow me instead; my dry skin, my stiff bones, I smell of pickled fish and remind you of lonely men, the world of handshakes and barren evenings. – Life laddie, life! A lonely activity on a nondescript road

TOM: Leading where?

DRY MAN: Away, always away

TOM looks at him in horror.

You're not with any of your bloody women now! You can feel disgusted all you want

The DRY MAN falls down in a fit. TOM watches, not knowing what to do.

Aren't you going to help me?

TOM: What can I do? You're mad. Look where your tough talking has got you. You're a cripple, a piss-soaked cripple

DRY MAN: A cripple is it? Don't let this fool you!

More convulsing.

What are you afraid of? You'll end up like this perhaps?

Come here (*His grip is iron strong.*) Taste this

He forces TOM to lick the corners of his mouth where the froth has formed.

TOM: Urgh! It's salt. Leave me alone!

DRY MAN: Salt you see, not foam, but salt. Salt, life!

TOM: I'm so thirsty. Let go!

DRY MAN: Why do you think Jesus was thirsty on the cross? Salt, salt! He was made to live a million salty lives in a few hours

TOM: No! It doesn't have to be like this. Life is sweet and young and full of love and light!

*   *   *

The DRY MAN is replaced by a party GUEST.

GUEST: So where are your friends and family now Tom? Eh? Not feeling lonesome are you? Come on back into the funeral party. It's all in your honour. Aren't you the one's made great advances in science and come up with the cures for all those diseases?

TOM: It is, Sir

GUEST: Don't be modest with me now Tom. Medicine is an important art, no-one can deny that... Of course disease too is a great leveller isn't it? It's a part of life and in all fairness where would we be without it?

TOM is looking round.

Are you looking for your wife Tom? Don't you worry about her now, come over and talk to the boys

MR COOMEY: ... you tell me why you're not funny any more?

MR HACKETT: Because I can no longer summon up the arrogance to laugh at others and I'm damned if I'm going to laugh at myself

COOMEY: Ah Tom, Mr Hackett was telling me you have some interesting thoughts on recent political developments

TOM: I wouldn't say that

HACKETT: We were just talking about our black friends, and the queers. Very problematic cases all in all

TOM: Well it's obvious you must subject the innocent victim to a good beating inspired by your worst prejudices. That way you know what they're really up against

COOMEY: He's a real scream isn't he?

BUBBLES: The most foul-mouthed braggart that ever carried a hod

TOM: I look inside at the commonplaces in my mind
and I wonder how life about me goes on unharmed;
the niggers and the queers, the bums and the jerks,
I expect them all to tumble to pieces in the aura of my
being. How I survive them and they me is a mystery

HACKETT: You sound like a jesuit. You are destined for greatness surely

TOM: I have insured myself against greatness by marrying a donkey

In the background his wife dressed in black tights and a top hat performs routine magic tricks in a matter of fact manner.

BUBBLES: She seems drunk, is she drunk?

GUEST: That priest, the one with the paintings, don't you think you might have offended him with your remarks on his work? He's gone off leaving them all behind

TOM: I said it to help him god damn him. I'll auction them. This one. Three hundred pounds!

COOMEY: Four. Five!

TOM: I think I started too low

BUBBLES: Six!

TOM: Stop Stop! I'm starting at a thousand

HACKETT: Your wife is taking her clothes off

TOM: Let her

COOMEY: She's a wonderful woman by the looks of her. Great shoes

HACKETT: (*To COOMEY.*) Not short of sixpence I can promise you

COOMEY: Men friends?

HACKETT: Men friends, women friends, friends of all descriptions

COOMEY: Who is that blighter in the big coat?

HACKETT: So you are the one with this strange phoenix. But I have heard it was not your discovery alone.

TOM: Not my discovery?

HACKETT: You've been spotted out by the rubbish bins whispering in corners with a dried up old man who, it is said, was walking around with a very similar gadget 40, 50 years ago. How do you like that?

TOM: I don't care for your speculations. You'll see nothing of this creature until it is already dead

HACKETT: Tell us, what does it do?

TOM: Nothing at all. Except...

HACKETT: Yes?

TOM: It speaks the truth.

HACKETT: A likely story. Where is it, let's hear it

TOM: As you should all know, truth is a shy virgin

COOMEY: I've tried Lao-tse, Kwang-tzu, Nietsche, Buber, Russell, Isiah Berlin, Isiah the prophet, Jung, Jesus, the I-Chin...

GUEST: You are drowning in a sea of wistfulness

COOMEY: No, I'm being eaten by the sharks of regret

BUBBLES: There they go with their metaphors

TOM: Who'll give me fifteen hundred?

BUBBLES: I feel drawn towards logical expression

HACKETT: It must be old age creeping on. Senility

COOMEY: ... punching walls, begging, pleading, stomping, shouting...

BUBBLES: (*To JULIE.*) Even the most useless person with no particular knowledge or talent – when they die and the contents of their heads are poured out, unexpected treasures will appear and you may say to their spirit "oh did you know that song? or remember that place?"

COOMEY: ... crying, lying, dirty weekends, writing letters, making friends, losing friends, library books, suspender belts, headache pills, falling in love, and I've even written a letter to the Queen protesting about the state of her prisons. And where did it all get me?

HACKETT: Where?

COOMEY: Nowhere. Bloody nowhere

BUBBLES: (*To JULIE.*) At least our children needn't all be Americans. They might be Sudanese

HACKETT: At least then they'll be able to read

GUEST: So at last the night nurse arrived and tended to my every need

BUBBLES: What a genius

COOMEY: (*To TOM.*) The major and minor poets, Irish, Jewish and downright English. I've tried sport, food, yoghurt, cigarettes, tea, cakes, stews, touching my toes, hot baths, sleep, tooth brushing, doctors, dentist, priest, watched the news, stayed at home, gone out, isolation, immolation, socialising, advertising, agoraphobia, claustrophobia, epilepsy, coke and pepsi, dark glasses, clean socks, buying plants, framing pictures –

BUBBLES: One of his eyelids was loose!

COOMEY: (*To TOM.*) Am I boring you?

BUBBLES: (*To GUEST.*) How is Louise?

GUEST: Mad as a hatter

HACKETT: My masturbation is a great source of jealousy to my wife. As well it ought to be

COOMEY: God I'm lonely

HACKETT: Ha! There was a time when I would have felt pity for you but nowadays everyone is lonely, everyone is upset, but ask them why they are upset and they can't tell you

JULIE: (*To BUBBLES.*) My reading? Mainly medieval history. And of course Eichendorf

HACKETT: Domestic life is difficult when an offer of tea is met with a glare of primal hatred

BUBBLES: (*To JULIE.*) No, don't write it at home, write it out here; stretched out on the sandy common

HACKETT: (*To COOMEY and TOM.*) I'm telling you politics to me is like reproduction to a tart. An unnecessary evil to be avoided

BUBBLES: (*To JULIE.*) If I exaggerate it's only in the cause of truth

COOMEY: He'd make a lousy tart wouldn't you think?

TOM: I don't know. (*He notices NELLIE and the PRIEST.*)

COOMEY: He keeps his spiritual legs firmly crossed

BUBBLES: Look why don't you just tell me who you vote for

HACKETT: (*To JULIE.*) Do you think he wants you eh? He doesn't want you!

COOMEY: You complain about your wife but just imagine if there was only the Exodus, the untrue, and the One who didn't believe you?

GUEST: The one who didn't believe me? When she departed all truth went out of my life

HACKETT: Give me a drink in the name of Jesus

In the background the PRIEST and NELLIE are dancing facing each other, pelvically.

TOM: Alright everyone time to go home, you're too drunk

BUBBLES: He's power mad

TOM: Why do all the women in this room have such a strong vaginal odour?

BUBBLES: This is Julie. Did you know she can actually see your aura? She's here about the rainforests aren't you dear?

TOM: Now Julie I'd guess you're the kind of girl's not wearing any knickers, am I right?

JULIE: I flew in this morning. I love airports don't you?
They're so 1950s

COOMEY: I'm sorry but I find the whole thing
embarrassing

GUEST: It would be alright if Tom weren't so obviously
showing off

*In the background TOM's wife is astride the PRIEST shouting the
slogan "Deep red sea, deep red sea" while he conducts her.*

HACKETT: Is that the cuckolds anthem I hear?

COOMEY: His greatest admirer once

HACKETT: No more it seems

TOM rushes up.

TOM: How dare you betray me in front of everyone
with a critic

*He slaps her clumsily catching her full on the nose. Instantly her face and
clothes are covered in blood.*

BUBBLES: I should say it serves him right

COOMEY: (*In a sour mumble.*) Critics. I wish I got paid for
slandering my betters

*   *   *

*The party GUEST leads TOM outside into the street, pulling on an
anorak, he is the DRY MAN.*

DRY MAN: I'd say you need some air. (*Leads him out.*)
So, the tragic balloon of optimism has burst

TOM: (*Who is a bit drunk.*) I'm too gentle and forgiving.
There's nothing like endless patience for provoking
cruelty. Do you have a wife?

DRY MAN: I do. The slut. She's living it up in gaol while
I'm stuck out here

TOM: You must miss her

DRY MAN: I do, but I have another. Don't you?

TOM: I certainly do thank Christ. Now she's awful nice to me. She orders me to stay. 'I need you' she says! 'I can't!' I said 'I'm pledged to another' and the door slammed in my face before I had time to step back inside for I had decided to stay

DRY MAN: What a laddoe! Not a thought for the consequences?

TOM: Love learns no lessons

The GIRL IN WHITE appears riding her bicycle.

GIRL IN WHITE: I do laugh when I think of you at a bus stop with your erection, comparing one human being to another!

TOM: Ha! And yet these are the ingredients and activities of love

GIRL IN WHITE: They are your only real achievements

TOM: At least I've come of age and no longer care for secrecy

GIRL IN WHITE: Though secrecy still cares for you, hiding your one thought from another, doesn't it?

DRY MAN: Ha, ha! Funny how when your marriage goes sour you can only keep alive your faith in love through adultery! Isn't that the irony of it!

TOM: Don't ask me to leave her and go on believing in love. How would I love you then? Would I then desert you too if you became ill like her and made me unhappy?

She lunges at him with a penknife, plunging it into his thigh, leaving it there. She rides away.

TOM: She buried her penknife in my thigh, I kept it there to her shame. Only years later did I allow her to draw it out

*   *   *

NELLIE hesitating at the gates of madness. She is stepping to and fro across the threshold of her bedroom.

NELLIE: ... they say the worst thing about being in prison is that you become your own gaoler. They will come and open the doors one day and I shall simply stare across the threshold

TOM: Yes, you say that and yet if I'm not mistaken you have the air of one with the travel fever...?

NELLIE: Yes, I'm going back to Germany. Here are my trunks, will you have them sent? You'll come with me later won't you?

TOM: With you? But I'm ill, I, I meant to tell you

NELLIE: You didn't mention it

TOM: You never gave me the chance. I have become a terror to myself, my body and soul are strangers to each other, my ears are blocked, my muscles are degenerating through underuse

NELLIE: Pull yourself together. Do you have any strong rope? Tie them all up, get them to the station, show your ticket, register the trunks for freight and that's it, done

TOM: I'll never manage. No second thoughts?

NELLIE: None. Sanity beckons – you recoil in horror. Goodbye darling. I'm already looking forward to you coming. We'll unpack it all together. Think, how happy we'll be

*   *   *

At his friend the PRIEST's house.

TOM: She's gone. I can't begin to tell you the tortures
I suffered at her hands

PRIEST: Was she cruel?

TOM: I like to say she was possessed

PRIEST: Then why so afraid of her going?

TOM: In a moment of weakness I resolved to take with
me my sick wife of no comfort. Like the insecure child
I take my inadequate mummy with me wherever I go

PRIEST: But it's not you travelling, it's her

TOM: So it is. Can you help me with these?

PRIEST: No damn you

*   *   *

The DRY MAN appears at his side.

DRY MAN: So your best friend says you have no backbone?

TOM: He curses me for my weakness to the same degree
that he worshipped me for my strength. He's nursing
his wounds

DRY MAN: Never let idolaters be your friends. You must let
them swear their allegiance, then run for it

TOM: He was strangely lacking in loyalty I thought...

DRY MAN: They idolise you so they can hate you,
blame you for everything that is wrong with themselves.
They seem to give you all power on earth but keep for
themselves the sacred power of resentment

TOM: You've a point there

DRY MAN: They will gather together in your name and
swear your destruction. And though you may sit at home

trembling, afraid to leave your four walls, or you may crawl meekly from tree to tree along a quiet street and be saying to yourself, consoling yourself, saying

In a quiet street.

TOM: I will go and see my friend for I am truly in need of a friend

DRY MAN: ... he will open the door snarling and say...

FRIEND: What do you come here for? Do you think I'm at your beck and call? To be visited when you feel like it? No, I want to be alone. You weakling. So you can't sweat it out by yourself, you thought you'd use me. Well don't come back, I'll see you in a year. To think I used to admire you, you spider!

Alone in the street.

TOM: So I did what I was told, and I did not go back even though the mound of suitcases on my floor tumbled perpetually up and down my stairs, left there by my wife for me to take to the station, the pile grew amid tangles of rope. Have you ever noticed the similarity between a trunk and a coffin?

And so heavy were they and so dizzy was I that I could not carry them and I went in sorrow to a certain person who opened her door and took me in her arms and fed me with blood from her broken heart. She carried my suitcases of her rival and buttoned my coat and said Goodbye Again, goodbye again, and all joy to her forever and ever and God forgive me for being loved

The GIRL IN WHITE rides past on her bicycle and waves "Bye".

DRY MAN: That's a touching story Tom. And shall we see how the man who loves to love, pays back this loyalty?

TOM: (*Modestly.*) No, no for God's sake I don't want that

DRY MAN: No go on, let's see it, because do you know what? I always find it so inspiring, as I'm sure she did, didn't she, bless her?

TOM, almost a magician, spreads his large wings in a protective sweep. With a masterful air he cues the wind of a storm.

A CHILD, aged six, trails in behind her mother, the GIRL IN WHITE.

CHILD: Mummy I feel funny again

The MOTHER stops, it's happening again. The CHILD goes into an epileptic trance, head to one side jerking slightly. TOM does battle with the disease.

TOM: I know you, I know exactly what to do. I will be here awake until the onslaught is over. With my second sight and my intuition I can see the enemy ranged against her fair head, and with the force of my heart I am outwitting it!

He stretches out his hands and grinds his jaws.

The CHILD falls back.

TOM: I know exactly what to do

The Mother gets the CHILD to its feet and leads it away.

TOM: I know exactly what to do

CHILD: Mummy...

TOM: Yes, I feel my powers returning

DRY MAN: Yes, you're a fine big man Tom Doheny. All your friends can rely on you, I can see that for sure

*   *   *

A street.

A man with a red face, in a dinner suit.

TOM: There, sit down on that wall and rest

DRY MAN: I fell down young fella and hit my head.
I might fall under a car. I've a pain in my chest and
all down my spine. Sure I know I haven't long to live

TOM: Have you been drinking?

DRY MAN: Of course I've been drinking. Give me your
little hand, oh God bless you it's half of mine, you're just
a little babbie. Feel that grip.

TOM: Formidable

DRY MAN: Don't worry I won't hurt you. Do you know
why? Because you're Irish. If you'd been anybody else
I would have taken your wrist, like this and done that,
like this, and your arm'd be broken

TOM: I think the ambulance is coming

DRY MAN: Did you call an ambulance? You little blighter.
I'm going to run away

TOM: Do you know Tom Clancy, he's a Cork man

DRY MAN: Shut up. I knew them all before you was even
born. They want me you know, they need a good man
with the dynamite, "only you can do it Tom Doheny"
they said. Oh Jesus me chest! Pins and needles in my
fingers too. Skin like bloody leather, I was out digging
ditches in the Yemen you know

TOM: Give me your hospital card, I'll show it to them when
they come. Is that you? Fine moustache

DRY MAN: Never mind the bloody moustache, that's me!
Feel that grip!

Ambulance arrives.

*   *   *

*A safe house. TOM has stolen the DRY MAN's identity. Three men
with black jackets.*

TOM: (*Holds up card.*) This is me, never mind the bloody moustache

ONE OF THE MEN: Only you can do it Tom Doheny...

TOM: There's going to be some re-thinking done here. Pure social bloody engineering. I've always been a strong believer in revolution

CELL LEADER: Take this, little man, and stop your blather (*Hands him a Kalashnikov.*)

*   *   *

Street corner. Hiding from an angry crowd.

CELL LEADER: Well Tom Doheny, that was a great thing, your social bloody engineering. Everyone's bloody dead to a man.

TOM: He who takes up the sword sends other people's sons to die by the sword.

CELL LEADER: And now their mammies are going to have your guts for garters for it, how d'ye like that?

A lynching band of murderous mothers approaches.

*   *   *

TOM is hanging upside down from a tree.

TOM: They hanged me upside down from a tree. No-one fed or watered me, I gave up the ghost. My friends, my so-called friends never came after me and so I presume they wish me good riddance

NELLIE appears alongside with the DRY MAN.

(*To NELLIE.*) And you! You see how you've poisoned everyone against me. (*He rails against her but his voice fades away.*) You always make a point of ducking when I swing my arms but I'm the one who's black and blue with the beatings you've given me, lord when I think of myself tears well up in my eyes...

NELLIE: He hung there for nine days. Wonderful. Made the worms and the slugs his brothers and sisters, that is; let what's at the bottom come to the top and what's topmost... fall out of his ears

TOM: I see you're not short of company

NELLIE: Yes I met this man, he's a great friend of yours isn't he? Why did you never introduce me to him?

TOM: (*Trying to hang with as much dignity as possible.*) Well at first I wasn't sure I could trust him

NELLIE: Ah Tom...

TOM: ... and now, I'm not sure he can trust me

NELLIE: Your political shenanigans didn't turn out too good did they?

TOM: Help me down from here now will ya?

NELLIE: Tom, you look like a fledgling fallen out of its nest. Is that what you meant by the magic bird?

*   *   *

Courtroom. TOM is in the dock doing a pile of ironing.

TOM: I find it difficult to believe that the God of love would involve us in this terrifying struggle against evil. I've learnt my lesson

PROSECUTION LAWYER: (*Indignant.*) But what about freedom of speech?

TOM: Freedom of speech is the prerogative of those on favourable terms with their publishers

The GALLERY cheer and he waves back, pleased.

... but if the world were up in arms against *my* book
I should withdraw it at once and serve them right!

GALLERY: *Boo*! No-one wants your rotten book anyway!

JUDGE: You have no principles, get on with your ironing

TOM: (*He retorts, braving the hecklers.*) The whole world is like a bad-tempered hedgehog, bristling with principles. Take pacifism for example, vastly overrated! It should only be used as a last resort

GALLERY: Hooray!

PROSECUTION LAWYER: But what about the defenceless victim?

TOM: Exactly. Who would begrudge him the chance of raising his knee into the groin of his attacker as he goes under? Who would even comment upon it, let alone say he had abandoned a principle.

Laughs from the GALLERY. TOM laughs coyly in reply.

PROSECUTION LAWYER: So you would resist tyranny at least

TOM: Hitler gave tyranny a very bad name

The crowd in the GALLERY boo. He rants in reply.

TOM: Now we have to stand up to them all, whatever the cost. Except the tyranny of hunger of course. It's the human face of the aggressor that attracts us, probably because he is our mirror image, like an angry dog we bark at it.

Applause.

PROSECUTION LAWYER: You speak from an ignorance of history no doubt.

The GALLERY laughs.

TOM: Just one mention of the word "history" and people are tossing babies into the air and shooting them

Dark murmurs from the GALLERY.

JUDGE: Let's not talk of war. Your ironing smells, you need that new freshener

A LONE VOICE IN THE GALLERY: (*Faintly.*) Whatever happened to old Tom Doheny?

JUDGE: I think you are a bit of a fascist

TOM: I know you do but my suburban friends think I'm very left wing... you might say to yourself 'do I know this man?' and you look at him and – sorry what were we talking about?

PROSECUTION LAWYER: You were having evil thoughts of mass destruction

TOM: I ask you, who has not? We lived in the shadow of the bomb and the consequent illiteracy for so long

GALLERY: Ha ha, listen to Tom the politician, look at the mouth on him, a mug of tea and he's anybody's man.

TOM: Death you see...

PROSECUTION LAWYER: Ah yes?

TOM: Death. Not understanding about life, how can you understand death?

PROSECUTION LAWYER: M'lud, the man's an imbecile

TOM: I... submit, let the son be the son, the father the father, the minister the minister, the ruler the ruler

JUDGE: (*Aside to the PROSECUTION LAWYER.*) What are you doing?

PROSECUTION LAWYER (*Scratching himself frantically.*) I have scabies m'lud.

TOM: I've had a lot of bad luck in my life. A friend of my wife's writes poison pen letters saying I am the enemy of life

A QUIPPER IN THE GALLERY: She wouldn't be far wrong there...

TOM: – but only last year this same person was wanting the two of us in bed at the same time!

JUDGE: (*Fascinated despite himself.*) Did you do it?

TOM: We both went round, but they made me do the washing up.

PROSECUTION LAWYER: Bad luck indeed. (*Winks to the jury.*) You didn't follow them to bed after your domestic duties were done?

TOM: Are you joking? They went off at eight o'clock, I never sleep before dawn. I need to see confirmed the promise of rebirth before I commit myself to the little death which is sleep

PROSECUTION LAWYER: You're afraid of the dark?

TOM: Who would trust the one who waves the flag of evil?

PROSECUTION LAWYER: You're hemming yourself in there

TOM: I know all about that

PROSECUTION LAWYER: You find blamelessness in your lethargy?

TOM: The intelligence of your questioning is rare

PROSECUTION LAWYER: Your self-disgust is an armoury against unpleasant surprises

TOM: Don't overdo it professor

PROSECUTION LAWYER: What would you say is your view of politics?

TOM: I object

JUDGE: Objection overruled

PROSECUTION LAWYER: Your view of politics

TOM: The sword of righteousness, the plough of good intent, the letterbox of hopefulness, the car of liberty, the mule of tourism, the mound of venus...

JUDGE: I'm not convinced

TOM: Love is impossible to explain, no-one understands

PROSECUTION LAWYER: (*In a sudden fit of anger.*) What goddam use are you?

TOM: The Lord said "make not strength a tool of your trade but weakness". Once I realised that I was well away. I became the mouth-piece of a nation. Not that that was any use to me

PROSECUTION LAWYER: No use you say and yet you did find some use for it did you not? In fact you were offered a mini-series

TOM: That's not true your worship. I tried to dredge up something but nothing was there! I had a hand full of trumps but no card to lead with

PROSECUTION LAWYER: M'lud, he's not answering the question

JUDGE: I must warn you that these weak arguments will gain you no favour with this court

TOM: I enjoy the spite of selecting the weakest arguments to express my case. It's a way of emphasising its self-evidency

JUDGE: (*Bitterly ironic.*) Very clever

The JUDGE places a black cloth on his head.

Take him down!

COURT USHER: The undersea kingdom awaits you sir, this way

TOM: God knows I was espoused to fearlessness as a youth! In fact I was so impressed by what she showed me that I ran straight from her into the arms of pure terror...

GALLERY: Whatever happened to old Tom Doheny?

TOM: ... in whose luxuriant embrace I shall languish until my dying day...

JUDGE: What a humiliating display, clear the court!

TOM: Destiny, that last great master of disguise offered me a trick and I fell for it!

JUDGE: What is the fellow talking about?

DEFENCE COUNCIL: (*Confidentially to the JUDGE.*) God's fool, the numbskull's right of intercession m'lud.

Riotous scenes as TOM DOHENY is led away.

*   *   *

The DRY MAN dressed unconvincingly as the undersea emperor leads TOM along through the weeds.

DRY MAN: Welcome to the undersea kingdom

TOM: You don't fool me, this is a field of turnips

DRY MAN: Nonsense. Didn't you see all those people we passed on our way waving their arms –

TOM: – Fists

DRY MAN: And that squireen that gave us a ride in his curricle.

TOM: You mean the squatter that threw us on the back with the pigs

DRY MAN: We'll get there. You'll see the sky clouded with seaweed

TOM: Oh to get out of here. I'd even beg forgiveness from my friends and family. Even the resentment of strangers would be a comfort –

DRY MAN: You see, above us only snow, below us African ground; this is the land of epitomes. Here it is no use to argue only to assuage. To be on the safe side call everything by its antonym, then everyone will understand

TOM: Is this where the Magic Bird comes into its own then?

DRY MAN: Not yet laddie, not yet. Learn to stand up on your own two feet, withered stumps though they be

TOM: You're joking I can tell. I've been dreaming. I shall wake up and it will be there again, I'll be home...

Home. TOM is in the bathroom wrestling NELLIE's head under the bath tap. She is in her magician gear, high heels, black tights, waistcoat, her top hat knocked off and rolling on the floor. He screams at her.

TOM: For God's sake let me get the blood off your face!

NELLIE: No! No!

Suddenly he sees a spider in the bath and screams in terror.

TOM: Urgh! a spider!

He hides behind his wife.

NELLIE: Where?

TOM: Kill it! Kill it! Get rid of it!

Suddenly, a man in an anorak with many arms grabs him around the neck and bites him.

Argh! Who the hell are you?

SPIDER: I'm the bloody spider

TOM: I always said they could bite, no-one believed me.
(*The vicious man-SPIDER has TOM's head in a lock and twists it while he raves.*)

SPIDER: You think you've got problems, my wife wants to eat me! You haven't known pain until you've begged for mercy and she's said 'I'll try'. It's not enough to cry your heart out, you must cut it out. But whatever you do with it thereafter it will always recognise birdsong, possibly as something malevolent but nevertheless familiar (*Twists harder.*)

TOM: Argh!

SPIDER: I open my mouth to utter the word 'freedom' and instead I say "close the door, close the door! hide me!" My head resounds with the clang of iron doors slamming. Each syllable has a thousand echoes

TOM: For God's sake, let go of me!

SPIDER: I look down in alarm at my hands to see they are clutching a spade digging my own grave, I turn to call for help but I find there only me, showing myself forward with a bitter sneer

TOM: I can't help you, please, I'm an arachnophobe

SPIDER: A dog runs at my heels and tries to bark but the poor brute can only whimper. I take pity on the dog and lower one of my hands to it but it tears at my fingers (*Bites his hand.*)

TOM: Argh!

SPIDER: My wife doesn't know what romance is, but she's begging to know

TOM: (*Choking.*) Is she?

SPIDER: I just hope she finds out in time

NELLIE now smacks the spider in the bath with her shoe she'd taken off and the man-SPIDER simultaneously falls backwards, dead.

NELLIE: Got it

In the turnip field once again.

TOM: Oh! (*He shivers and trembles with disgust.*)

DRY MAN: Don't you worry lad, I'll show you something new each day and when you're an old man you'll look back on your life of experience and adventure and you'll say "I've lived"

TOM: But who shall I say it to?

DRY MAN: Some distant guardian of a distant gate. There'll always be someone there to light your way, have faith

TOM: (*In terror.*) No, no! please help me, what can I do?

DRY MAN: Alright, I'll tell you. This is it: Go and see a doctor, say to him, "doctor I've –

TOM is in a doctor's surgery.

TOM: – lost my nerve

DOCTOR: So have I. Lost it long ago. That's why I'm sitting here. I gave up everything to be where you see me now. As you get older you make it impossible for yourself to see or hear anything new. The day is filled with things familiar to you until at last you feel you know your way about in this life, at that point you should realise you have surrendered to decay. And as you struggle to achieve the symbolic goal you have set yourself to convince you of your gameness, you desperately struggle to keep the balloon aloft by jettisoning ballast. This ballast though is Life Itself, you leave it behind you, strewn across the landscape of your unlived past. And the more you throw out, the lower the balloon sinks. Close your eyes, stand on one leg

TOM: (*Does so.*)

DOCTOR: Solid as a rock

Turnip field.

TOM: Actually as a matter of fact, now you mention it, Lights out.we go onwards and onwards but each day you get sicker

DRY MAN: (*Foaming at the mouth.*) Poor auld Tom Doheny, he thought up the magic bird, a cure for all ills upon us currently and he professed it until he became a fool. "alas"

TOM: ... he said...

DRY MAN: ... the Magic Bird is dead, my intentions are dust and I must follow behind. Remember me

TOM: But you had so many important things to say, where are they all?

DRY MAN: Lost in my desire to be your slave little man

TOM: If my friends could see me now

DRY MAN: (*Hiding his irony.*) Yes, yes, it's a great victory for you

TOM: I quite enjoy this world you brought me into

DRY MAN: The womb awaits you. Take me back with you

TOM: No, no, this is wonderful. I've never in my life experienced one moment of abandon. But now I'm going to drink this

TOM drinks the sea.

DRY MAN: (*In horror.*) You madman! You liar! You've drunk my undersea kingdom dry!

TOM: Puny liquor it is too. And me almost a tee-totaller

At once they are at sea.

TOM: In a trice we are riding a foamy wave on the green ocean under a blue sky

DRY MAN: It has its downside you know

TOM: Don't tell me life has any limitations for the departing spirit. Suddenly you're staring freedom in the face

DRY MAN: Don't remind me, liberty's crumbling dental arrangements have been grinning at me since I was in shorts

TOM: ... look at the gulls in our wake

DRY MAN: ... hungry blighters

TOM: ... flapping those giant wings of theirs

DRY MAN: ... I wish they wouldn't, they're working up a wind

TOM: ... in fact, hold on, they're whipping up a storm

DRY MAN: ... those damn birds!

TOM: Hold on, we're going home. Who's that calling out below?

On board ship in a heavy sea. TOM DOHENY.

JACK TAR: It's not the sea that galls us Tommy with it's hearty tossing, it's you aloft in your underpants in the crow's nest all "land ahoy" and hopefulness. Your indominability in the face of certain death reminds us of the orphanage. Come down from there, there's a little thing we'd like to whisper in your red old ear that might interest you

TOM: Call out if you've something to say, I think I spy land

'SWAIN: (*Shouting above the foam.*) Well, we don't want to embarrass you but there's an old pig down here says you're his father. In the circumstances we'd like you to come and answer the charge of bestiality

TOM: God damn yous! My life has been a long one, I can't remember every detail

'SWAIN: It's not the obscenity in the normal sense that troubles us Tommy but you see it's the thought of your seed being wasted on dumb animals, we all... we all feel a bit insulted, don't we lads, especially the girls amongst us

TOM: Is that a fact?

JACK TAR: It is Tommy, it is. Come down and meet your son

A PIG: (*Snorts and grunts eagerly from below.*)

TOM: I will not. Don't you all want to be saved from this terrible storm?

AN OLD SALT: No it's alright, we're all insured

TOM: (*Insulted.*) Oh. Didn't you trust your captain?

JACK TAR: How could we, with that old crow wrapped around your shoulders?

TOM: This is the Magic Bird

AN OLD SALT: It's dead

TOM: Dead but clinging on nevertheless

AN OLD SALT: Get that ill-omened carcass out of there or we'll make you walk the plank

TOM: You mutinous scoundrels! I'm the boss around here. You're forgetting perhaps who made this leaking hulk what it is today. You were nothing more than a glorified pleasure skiff full of ditch water until I took command. Now it will take the very eye of this typhoon to wreck us

UNDERSEA EMPEROR: Ah let the poor deluded navvy sit up there if he wants to. What difference is it to us anyway, we're doomed men

TOM: Watch out below, there's some big seas coming! There's one wave... and there's another

ALL ABLE BODIED SEAMEN AS ONE: Oh Merciful God!

TOM: Let's see where your blackmailing pigs will get you now (*He laughs boldly as the seas overwhelm his ship.*)

JACK TAR: You wicked paddy! Why are you taking us to our destruction? We've been your hearties all this long trip, why pick on us?

TOM: Ah it's a different tune now you're singing. Ha ha! (*The sea rolls.*) We'll all go together! Hang on to your bulwarks!

The wild seas rage, TOM DOHENY laughs aloft.

UNDERSEA EMPEROR: I'll get him down, I'll get him (*Scales the mizzen.*) You wild man, I'll pull you down by God!

TOM: Ah who's that down there, ha! the undersea emperor no less! So you'd scale my mizzen mast would you? Take that!

He swipes at him with the carcass of the MAGIC BIRD.

MAGIC BIRD: (*Squawks vainly.*)

UNDERSEA EMPEROR: Your squawking carcass doesn't scare me boy!

The UNDERSEA EMPEROR achieves the summit, they fight.

Now my blue-bearded rascal, got you! (*He has him round the neck.*) Why don't you allow yourself the luxury of admitting you have always been hopelessly and undeniably a liar and a cheat, a blind beggar on the road to hell!

TOM: I cannot accept your last generous offer. You alone are to blame for the wicked perversion of my miserable life

UNDERSEA EMPEROR: I'll dislodge you from your perch, you and your monstrous parrot

TOM: If I go you'll go with me! and we'll drown together in the white-crested darkness of the sea

UNDERSEA EMPEROR: Let it be so!

They topple away, locked in mortal combat.

*   *   *

Washed ashore, discovered on the beach by his old friend, the PRIEST.

TOM: You think I'm sunbathing but in fact I'm shipwrecked and washed up upon the shore

PRIEST: (*Mumbles something in reply.*)

TOM: Where are my friends? They're strewn about here somewhere. At least they all came with me even if few survived the trip. They were all sea-faring men, God bless them. A refreshing change I can tell you after a life of landlubbers and Judases

PRIEST: Don't you want to know where you are?

TOM: It's all the same to me, my life is near its end, I have
but a few words left to utter, a few scenes left to play. My
repertoire is down to several wan smiles and a little wave
(*He waves feebly.*) like this

PRIEST: Why man, you're drunk

TOM: Yes! Ha! Yes indeed, my senses were stolen by the
chateaux fonds of the lower vineyards. But excuse me do
you know my wife? She'll want to know, she always
wants to know, her love is such she will want to know

He looks out to the surf.

The sea, the sea, the roving sea, charms my destiny.
Loneliness hangs upon me like an anchor chained on a
cliff face

DISTANT VOICE: Whatever happened to old Tom
Doheny!

PRIEST: You're in a fine state aren't you?

TOM: My dear fella, you're a priest but there's no romance
in your soul. I may have grown a beard and put on
unfamiliar clothes but I am the same man underneath

PRIEST: ?

TOM: I may have changed my mind and changed my heart
but I am the same man underneath

PRIEST: If not a heart or a mind what is a man? No more
than a stomach

TOM: Then I am the same stomach

PRIEST: Tell me do your old friends recognise you?

TOM: Recognise me? They never knew me in the first place

PRIEST: A man who cannot trust his friends is a man with
a mean nature

TOM: Or mean friends

PRIEST: And your family, have they welcomed you back?

TOM: Surely. They sent money for my ticket and begged me to come home. Now of course they ignore me. You can't expect miracles. Anyway at least it was a touching scene as the bigot rescued me from my persecutors

PRIEST: What? You faced a mutiny?

TOM: The boat I was on sunk many times. Waves as big as houses engulfed us time after time. Prayer was futile, there was nothing for it but to man the pumps

PRIEST: Ah I am no stranger to the bilges myself. The ship's biscuit and the holy sacrament have been the twin cakes of my sustenance on this earth

TOM: Who ever heard of a priest on the yard arm. A clergyman at sea is useless. Rather than binding his wrists to the wheel he would rather strap himself to the mast in imitation of his master. I must leave you now and write a letter. The hour prior to sleep is my best writing hour. I strap myself to the mast of my pen while the waves of my unconscious rise up about me. I awake in the morning to see the inky measure of their wrath on the page beside me

PRIEST: Is it any wonder she despises you. She wants a highway in the sand, you give her shipwrecks from your pillow

*   *   *

An old BIDDY talking to herself. A familiar bicycle is leaning against the wall. She is tending geraniums in pots.

BIDDY: ... and then there's loads of dem dere don't want to work, mind over matter or whatever you may call it...

A passionate plea comes from old TOM in a wheelbarrow wheeled by the PRIEST.

TOM: Tell her, tell her for God's sake. She may laugh at these stained vest and pants now but in our youth she was glad enough of them, couldn't keep her chapped fingers out of them as I recall. Those red rings round her eyes were once moist fairy rings of delight. For God's sake woman what good is there in leaving it like this?

BIDDY: Oh John-Joe how I loved thee!

TOM: Get off, get off, I'm not him! You liar, you old braggart! We won't trouble your ladyship just let us rest here awhile in your roses

BIDDY: Rest there all you like, you can bury yourselves underneath 'em for all I care. They need a good peating

TOM: Oh so you see me as a source of manure now. There was a time... So if here amongst your roses I remain, anyway you'll not be long for this world...

BIDDY: (*To PRIEST.*) Tell me sir, is it a meal you're begging? For I've some old stew in a can I could bring out, save him bothering the neighbours with his chanting

TOM: Stew is a magnificent thing to be sure, but we were hoping for something a little more vital

BIDDY: Not forgiveness I hope

TOM: No, not that. Not that but recognition

BIDDY: Recognition you may have and take away with you all you may find and never come back with it, so I can live peacefully and forget all about it

TOM: She doesn't understand a word we're saying. Surely you have some recollection woman of the love we shared together

BIDDY: Huh, how could I forget, wasn't it that put me here to rot forever on my own?

TOM: Precisely, precisely, which is why madam I have
    come to join you now, Christ she's slow on the uptake

PRIEST: Tom, this isn't getting us anywhere, let's move on

TOM: God damn you! I may have misled you, deserted
    you, abandoned you, robbed you of happiness, left you
    to lead a life of lonely sorrow and deprived you of any
    children we might have had, but you couldn't say
    I haven't loved you!

BIDDY: Call that love!

TOM: And what do you call this? The scar on my thigh
    where you plunged your knife

BIDDY: (*Peers.*) All I see is a mass of grey hairs (*She weeps,
    strokes his leg.*) Oh Tom, Tom what a fine leg you always
    had! I never could look at your shabby body without
    wanting you!

They embrace with tears.

TOM: Ah Bridget, Bridget, my own sweet girl what has
    happened your hair? She was as gold as the dawn from
    head to foot. And you're as fat as the bog itself.

BIDDY: I told you I'd grow round like a ball, I like it

TOM: Oh so do I, so do I!

BIDDY: Come on round the back with me now and I'll lift
    my skirts for you like I used

She disappears.

TOM: I must go with her

PRIEST: (*Helps him to hesitate.*) You can't go in your vest.
    Hadn't you better borrow my big coat?

TOM: What would I be wanting a coat for?

PRIEST: To take off. You must have something to take off for the full effect, to sweep her up in, they like to be swept up and those thin arms of yours won't be doing much sweeping will they?

TOM: After all these years. Not a night has gone by that I haven't longed for her. My throat has gone all sticky with the thought of her

PRIEST: Why dally then, off you go

TOM: Because she always cries so sorrowfully every time, it breaks my heart to see her. And then she drifts away, looking over my shoulder and I'm left alone like a fool

PRIEST: You're afraid of the great well of emotion inside her

TOM: Nonsense, I'm not afraid of that, I can match her. God we used to roll around when we were young, you wouldn't credit it. And laugh! by Christ. And I'll tell you one thing, I have paid in suffering for every moment spent with her, I've no debt to pay on that score

PRIEST: Go on then she's waiting

TOM: I'll bet she's as hot now as she was then

PRIEST: I'll bet

TOM: It was something came entirely natural to her like breathing

PRIEST: She was certainly the girl for you sounds like

TOM: For me? Oh God she was never mine. Never, never mine. Or was she? In a sense she was. And still is. There is a secret bond to be sure, in a dimension invisible to the men and women of this earth

PRIEST: A bond of immense joy

TOM: And immense sorrow

PRIEST: If you take her now maybe she'll be yours forever

TOM: Oh no, you don't know her, she's a fierce girl, oh yes don't worry about that, she'll not be giving herself for nothing no more, she's tried that and was bitterly burnt. I could no more have her for my own than I could the hills over there or the rivers that run between

PRIEST: Independent is she?

TOM: What? Go and ask her and she'll give you a thick ear for your trouble. No men will ever come near her, no man in my opinion is good enough to even sit and drink her watery tea (her tea which I grant is filth). She has the dignity of a tigress and the sweetness of a cub, the shoulders of a venus, the mouth of a fish, the breath of a whore, the eye of a poem, the foot of a cripple, the breast of a dove, the nose of a navvy, the heart of an oyster, and I am a herring, do you hear me a herring, floating headless on its back, this way and that on the ocean's tides...

PRIEST: I can see you're too in love to function. Would you like me to go and tell her?

TOM: Never, never! I've not failed her yet and I won't now. Just give me a help out of this wheelbarrow

Does so.

BIDDY: (*Reappearing.*) It's no good Tommy, I can't go through with it, it will leave me red and raw like it always did and I don't want to feel the pain of loss today of all days no thankyou for I have other troubles

TOM: You've always had your troubles my love and it kills me that I cannot help you

BIDDY: It kills me too but there it is. You'll have to go now, my child is sick and I must away to her with some herbs

TOM: Is there any way I can help you, any way at all?
I hate to see you labouring, you look tired and drawn

BIDDY: That's nothing but age. Off with you now. Come
back soon and see me and don't look so sorrowful

They stagger away.

TOM: Enough of despondency – Now of exhilaration, come
I'll show you a fine thing

He stops.

I now realise that you will find my pleasures are only
weaknesses indulged to the point of enjoyment but, I ask
you... oh well here she comes...

*NELLIE appears dressed in a top hat and high heels. Comes and
performs a sullen magic trick with extreme grace. Her cane turns to a
handkerchief then to a dove, fluttering wings accompanied by a clanking
piano.*

PRIEST: Why that's amazing!

TOM: This is Nellie, you remember her

PRIEST: Of course

TOM: She has promised to teach me tricks too. Haven't you

She smiles but not in response to his question.

PRIEST: She's very beautiful

TOM: Make us all disappear

Does so.

LAZY BRIEN

Characters

LAZY BRIEN

MA

SUMPTER

GOAT

JOHNJO

NARRATOR

LAZY BRIEN was first performed on BBC Radio in 1993. It was directed by Eoin O'Callaghan, with the following cast:

LAZY BRIEN, Gerard McSorley

MA, Margaret D'Arcy

SUMPTER, Sheelagh O'Kane

GOAT, Brigid Erin Bates

JOHNJO, Joe McPartland

NARRATOR, Kevin Flood

A tiny cottage in Ireland. The racket of animals outside.

NARRATOR: In a tiny cottage in Ireland a young lad called Brien was lying fallow on his mother's floor, stretched out in the dust, a willing doormat in search of repose

MA: It's time to take the goat out to grass

BRIEN: No, mammy. I can't. I have a dream I must finish off. Why didn't you bring a bucket of grass for the brute back with you when you went washing your old drawers by the river

MA: You want your mother to do all the work

BRIEN: And why not? If you didn't work you'd be miserable and bitter, your muscles would wither on your bones

MA: I'll wither your little bones son with my boot if you don't move out of that and take the poor goat to feed

BRIEN: Alright mammy if that's your tone, I'll do it. But I'll only take her to the gate and let it run its own way

MA: It'll be killt by a farmer if you do that

BRIEN: What harm will that be to us? He'd be forced to pay us compensation for the goat and with the money you can buy a cheaper goat and we'll live on the profits and laugh to ourselves

MA: And what if the cheaper goat were a poor one and gave no milk, what then?

BRIEN: Then we'd kick it to death and eat it and think no more of goats or their fierce tasting milk or their grazing or their ridiculous beards and their horns

MA: What you are describing is a billy goat

BRIEN: Spare me the details. I've never looked

Grunting and groaning as he rises and goes to the door.

MA: By Christ you're not clever son are you!

BRIEN: No mother, I'm as stupid as you are and may I ever remain so

He goes out through the rickety door.

MA: Look at him! Go on away, further, further! He's stopped at the little wicket gate. Step over it you lazy good-for-nothing. Look at the poor goat straining at his tether, her grey old tongue hanging in the dust. Go on you shirker! Get out into them fields. Ah at last, he's turned the corner

Sits down and weeps from exhaustion. The rickety door is given a hefty shove from without. FAT 'SUMPTER waddles in huffing and puffing from the strain of manoeuvering her great bulk.

NARRATOR: No sooner had the tears of exhaustion moistened her wrinkled cheeks than the rickety door was shoved open and the neighbour, Fat 'Sumpter waddled in, a young girl, the scarcity of whose qualities were more than redeemed by her generous bodily quantity.

SUMPTER: Hello old mother

MA: Good day to you Fat 'Sumpter. Did you see my son?

SUMPTER: I did

MA: Was he taking the goat far out into the fields or was he dithering on the corner just out of sight of his own front door?

SUMPTER: Why are you forever asking questions. God, was I born to answer that kind of interrogation? I told you I'd seen him, I didn't stand gazing after him as he went his way did I? I'd be forever spinning my head around if I went about that way Old Mother. I'd get red sores on my neck from my old chemise that would be chafing and giving me all sorts of problems. I'd have to go down to the river and be bathing my neck out of all necessity and I'd end up with damp clothes and wrinkled fingers and a twisted spine from bending to reach down into the shallows for the warmer water all just to catch sight of your loitering son who never did harm nor good to any neighbour, old man or young girl

MA: Ah go on, for all your talking I can tell you're sweet on him

SUMPTER: Your son? What interest would he arouse in a woman?

MA: He is a man after all

SUMPTER: Let him prove it

MA: He would if you showed him encouragement

SUMPTER: What? Am I to stand winking and waving out in the street or beckoning him from my doorway. Is that your plan?

MA: No, no, you'd shame your parents

SUMPTER: Maybe if I lifted my skirt or smiled?

MA: He was very grateful that time you pulled one of his teeth.

SUMPTER: It was already hanging on a thread. Either he was too weak to have it out himself or he wanted my fingers in his mouth. Probably the latter for he was bent on sucking the very dirt from under my nails and wouldn't let go until they were on the verge of decomposing in his mouth

MA: He's a strange boy, but affectionate wouldn't you say?

SUMPTER: Are you trying to make me take him? You think I'm fat and none of the healthy-minded lads would like me. I promise you I've had more offers than I can count

MA: Yes, praise your good fortune that simple labouring men like a woman of good substance and don't go in for the other arrangements. But admit you are not only vastly overweight but you are also as lazy a slut as ever darkened a plain wooden door

SUMPTER: What of that? I'll not argue with you for I know you to be a cunning deceiver like all thin old hags. You're always on your way to proving some theorem or other to pull the wool over the eyes of the unsuspecting

MA: Your mother says there are days when you barely move and she has to push you out of the house with a strong stick

SUMPTER: My eyes are shy of the light

MA: Your fingers are shy of the hoe more like. Don't you think I don't know why you're here. You'll be wanting some free milk from our goat

SUMPTER: Perhaps I do. Would you have your neighbours starve for the want of a drop of milk to moisten their lips with

MA: No surely, take all you want, only leave enough for my son and myself, for though he is as worthless as a spokeless wheel drawn by a legless carthorse I'd not have him parched or undernourished even if it meant the surrounding fields would become vast graveyards to cater for the corpses of my close neighbours. Let 'em all drop in their tracks is what I say to them

SUMPTER: It's only a little splash in the bottom of my old jug I want. I brought my own stoup

MA: No, use ours

SUMPTER: But my own is bigger

MA: I'm well aware of it, here

SUMPTER: You have the cunning of an ant, old woman

MA: God bless you child, you're no dolt yourself. Listen Fat 'Sumpter, wouldn't it be grand and also great common sense for you and Brien to marry one of these Sundays?

SUMPTER: What would I be wanting to throw my lot in with him for?

MA: Can't you imagine the calm undisturbed life you'd have together?

SUMPTER: May I take another stoup of milk, my jug isn't quite filled

MA: Yes, but don't spill drips on the floor. You could lay abed together the live long day dreaming up ways to preserve energy and turn your sloth to gold, with your two great intelligences harnessed to each other, like. You're the inspiration he needs

SUMPTER: Oh really. Do you think so? May I take another stoup, for I think my jug may lose some over the wide old brim on the way home

MA: Yes, watch that dribble running down the side there. Catch it with your thumb, that's it. I'm sure the two of you would go great guns. Great guns

SUMPTER: Yes well, I can't say I've ever looked at it in that way to tell you the honest truth

MA: Ah, a mother has the foresight of thousands when it comes to paving the way for her little ones. Why don't you think about it on your way home with that jug and let me know when you return with your mother's old

clay pot, because I'm sure she'd like to see a few drops of
our milk in that to relieve the awful dryness of it

SUMPTER: It would indeed soften the blow of the
onslaught old age has made upon her. I'll be back in
a minute

MA: That's it 'Sumpter, that's it

Lazy BRIEN returns. He and FAT 'SUMPTER meet in the doorway.

BRIEN: Oh, hello Fat 'Sumpter. Isn't that the fine day

SUMPTER: It is Lazy Brien, it is

She goes off, squelching across the muddy yard.

BRIEN: Yes, mother I'm back early, and it's on account
of the goat herself who wouldn't stop tugging at her
rope and chafing my fingers. And I thought to myself:
Sure wouldn't the animal be far better off tied to a
post on the corner.

MA: That's alright son

BRIEN: It is? Well Mammy, of course I will try to
remember what corner it was so you'll have no trouble
when you go out to fetch her at sundown.

MA: That's considerate of you Brien. Did you see Fat
'Sumpter in the doorway?

BRIEN: I saw little else for she blocked the light with her
great bulk

MA: Yes, she's a fine strong girl. I see you have a good eye
for a person's qualities son. I suppose that must be a
consequence of your contemplations on the floor there

BRIEN: I expect it is, yes

MA: God forgive me, it must be a terrible hardship to have
the likes of your old mother chattering in your ear from

morning to night, and you being the type that prefers a silence to aid your thinking

BRIEN: Ay, you have a good point. Let me lie down now awhile. Your talking has exhausted me

MA: Wouldn't it be a great thing if you were to have a house of your own where you could persue your interests

BRIEN: (*Sleepily.*) Yes, but who would cook my food and bring it to me?

MA: A wife of course!

BRIEN: A wife!

MA: Some good-natured girl with no suggestion of the flibberty-jibbet about her who wouldn't be running about after the handsome men with her big shoes on her and a yellow wig or whatever they get up to these days

BRIEN: Well mammy, of course...

MA: And of course a girl with the same restful inclinations as youself but, what shall I say, not quite as entirely restful as it might be called a sickness like in yourself, but a girl who would, for example, be glad to walk a goat without any extra need of persuasion

BRIEN: But where would I find such a creature?

MA: Have you never noticed the way Fat 'Sumpter is always standing at her window from breakfast 'til supper each day trying to get a glimpse of you?

BRIEN: I have not. And anyway she'd be unlikely to catch sight of me those early hours

MA: But that's the beauty of it. She's no idea what a complete waster you really are. Not that she'd care, for she's that sweet on you, bless her. And wasn't she here today saying how she'd like to take the goat out to graze

BRIEN: Curses! Was she? If only I had lingered a while longer she could have taken it and I could have stayed at home

MA: True, but think what it would be to have her always to take out the goat for you. I'd let you have the goat, and you'd be working less than ever

BRIEN: Mother forgive me if, in the past, I have called you an old biddy with the mentality of a blind ox. This is well thought out. Except... she'd never agree to it

MA: Don't you believe it for here she comes across the yard swaying like a galleon on a heavy sea and by the little white trickle on her grey chin I'd say she's gone and swallowed all the milk I've given her. If you'd stand up you'd see her drunk with the thought of all the free milk

BRIEN: But what's that terrible noise? She's rattling like a tinker!

MA: It's all the pots and pans she's carrying. She's brought everything she could find. It's a good job she's a strong pair of arms for she must have a mine of copper tied onto her belt

Clattering and clanking as FAT 'SUMPTER comes in.

SUMPTER: Hello good mother. I brought my old Mammy's couple of old pots like you said

MA: Fill away, fill away, mind Brien on the floor there, you nearly stepped on his head. He's resting after his exertions

SUMPTER: Hello Brien

BRIEN: Hello 'Sumpter, you're looking fine if I may say so, and none the worse for the majestic sweep of your old black skirt that hangs about your calves. Bless me

I could easy get used to watching you stride over me the way you did. My senses are wafted to heaven by your scent as you passed across me. You're a fine girl

SUMPTER: Stop your blathering and hold on to this while I scoop the milk into it

BRIEN: But I can't reach

SUMPTER: Just steady it then with your foot, that's it. You've a fine strong toe there I can see. Hold on now

Clattering and sploshing as the milk is poured.

MA: Ah sure it melts a mother's heart to see when the young start their courting. If you'd move your posterior 'Sumpter 'til I squeeze past. I'll go into the yard and leave yous to it. (*Goes.*)

SUMPTER: ... Hold that bucket still with your blasted foot. Don't be spilling the milk down that excuse for a leg of yours!

BRIEN: Hold your whist!

NARRATOR: With these words and others like them Brien and 'Sumpter forged a bond of affection and trust that led irresistably to that imperishable partnership – Marriage

*   *   *

Inside the new marital home of BRIEN and SUMPTER, a creaky old shed with wind whistling through the rotten slats.

BRIEN: I hate to be complaining but God love me I haven't had a day's rest since I married you

SUMPTER: Is that my fault? I'm weak with the hunger. I can't do a thing. Did I know you wouldn't be able to support me?

BRIEN: But sure it's a task for ten men to feed you

SUMPTER: Feed me. You couldn't satisfy the appetite of a chicken with typhoid

BRIEN: It's not for the want of trying. I'm destroyed with the labour

SUMPTER: All you've done is walk up the hill to your mother and bring back her leftovers, while I'm stuck in this old shed with just barely room to lie down in it

BRIEN: You want to count yourself lucky it's not standing room only. And while you're out with the goat now I'm going to have a stretch out and digest my breakfast

SUMPTER: That's what you think. I've a plan, we're selling that goat

BRIEN: But where will we get milk?

SUMPTER: I don't plan to live out my days pouring that slimey muck down my gullet

BRIEN: What else will we dip in the sour bread that mammy lets us have?

SUMPTER: Honey, sweet, lovely honey

BRIEN: Honey? From bees like?

SUMPTER: By Christ Brien you're a scholar. There's a man over the hill keeps bees. We'll swap him the goat for a beehive. Then all we have to do is let the bees make honey for us, scoop it out with a spoon and eat it

BRIEN: Mammy was right, you were the inspiration I needed

SUMPTER: So off you go now, if you hurry you'll be back by sundown

BRIEN: What?

SUMPTER: It's only a few miles. You can lean on the goat if you get tired

BRIEN: You're not suggesting that I go wandering the countryside executing your hairbrained schemes are you woman?

SUMPTER: I'll tell you what'll I do. You go get the beehive from the gentleman and I'll clear a little patch outside by the window where we'll put it when you get back

BRIEN: Hold onto me 'Sumpter, my legs are failing me

SUMPTER: ... And if you don't I'll skin your puny body and make a jacket for the poor goat from your hide so I get a better price for it on my own

BRIEN: You're a violent woman. It's a cowardly thing to be using your abnormal physical strength to threaten your husband. If I were half your size I'd have a go at you

SUMPTER: You wouldn't stand a chance

BRIEN: What wouldn't I give for a decent spade with what to level the high plateau of your shoulders with

SUMPTER: I'll give you a high plateau out of the door if you don't stir your stinking carcass

She beats him and ejects him through the rickety door.

BRIEN: Alright I'm going

*   *   *

NARRATOR: So Brien set off up the hill on his errand, struggling through the weather, leading the slow goat and muttering to himself...

BRIEN: What kind of a wife would throw her husband out into the bitter wind and the rain? Look at that road stretching out ahead, sure my thin legs will never make that. I'm going to have to sit down and rest for a minute

NARRATOR: Worn out by the toil of walking and talking simultaneously, poor Brien was compelled to get down

and rest and he took up position in the ditch like
a little wayside flower and began to fall asleep, drowsily
fending off the goat's hungry advances

*He settles himself down. The goat bleats contentedly then starts chewing.
The goat is at his boots.*

BRIEN: Go on away out of that you old goat. What're you
eating my boots for when there's all this lovely green
grass. You stupid beast, if I had the energy I'd give you
a good kick in the molars, that would stop your ravenous
inroads on my shoes by God, but, as it is... I haven't the
strength to lift my leg so... eat away. And may it choke
you

*The goat chews heartily, ripping the soles off BRIEN's shoes. Later,
a contented bleating from the goat and a heavy snoring from BRIEN.
An owl hoot. A few drops of rain splash down.*

*   *   *

NARRATOR: And no sooner was Lazy Brien asleep
than it seemed he must prise open his eyes again.
But though the early birds were raucously screeching
their morning song, the raising of his heavy lids
revealed only darkness

Morning bird song. The GOAT belches.

BRIEN wakes up. His voice comes somewhat muffled.

BRIEN: (*From within the goat.*) Yawn. It must be morning, but
by Lucifer it's a dark one. Where is that goat? Where are
you hiding you mangy brute?

GOAT: What do you mean where am I, I'm here. Where are
you?

BRIEN: I can't see you. This bloody weather – I can't see a
thing

GOAT: That's because I've eaten you all up

BRIEN: What?

GOAT: You're inside my stomach. I think I must have faltered in the chewing department, the taste was so atrocious, I was forced to swallow the most of you whole

BRIEN: You stupid animal, whatever did you eat me for, I'm your master

GOAT: You never fed me, I was hungry

BRIEN: O Jesus! What'll I do now??

GOAT: Well how do you think I like it, having an undigested lump in my guts. (*Burps.*) Cripes, you're playing havoc with my intestines, sit still!

BRIEN: How will I get out! What a terrible fate to befall a man!

GOAT: You should look on the bright side, you won't ever have to walk again. I can hardly stand up with the weight of you

BRIEN: Fair play to you, there's truth in that. But it's darker than hell in here and it stinks like a drayman's drawers

GOAT: Keep your remarks to yourself. Look, I'll open my mouth for you, let in a little light. How's that?

BRIEN: A bit better. Urgh! What unspeakable meals have you been eating?

GOAT: What we goats call the glories of the wayside. And your own shoes of course, they certainly have the whiff of luxury about them don't they?

BRIEN: We can't stand here in the road all day like a couple of egits

GOAT: Hold your whist now, help is on its way. There's an old cart coming over the hill with a little fella on top of it

BRIEN: What'll we say to him?

GOAT: I'll not say a thing

BRIEN: Why not?

GOAT: What would I be talking for, I'm a goat

BRIEN: You're talking now

GOAT: It was the shock of hearing a voice from my stomach made me do it. You talk to him

BRIEN: Alright, but I feel like a great fool

A cart jingle jangles along. Stops.

JOHN JOE: Woa! Well, well, well, well, well, well, well. A old goat on its own. I'll take it home with me, I will, I will sure, I'll take it home. It'll be my own goat, it will, my own goat, C'mon you let me get this rope around your neck

BRIEN: Just you wait a minute now, hold your horses. Where are you taking me?

JOHN JOE: God preserve us it speaks

BRIEN: That's right Seamus, this is a talking goat, so you'd better watch out

JOHN JOE: I will, sir, I will, I was only thinking you were an old goat like, so that I'd take you home and feed you, sure. I didn't mean no harm your Lordship (*To himself.*) It's the devil himself

BRIEN: I'll not go home with you. Take me to Fat 'Sumpter's place down in the gulch, do you know it?

JOHN JOE: I do sir

BRIEN: Then get on with it. But you'll have to throw me up on the back of your cart, cause I'll not walk, I'm bloated

JOHN JOE: No sir, you'll not need to do any walking with me sir I've a fine cart here, a fine cart, We'll, we'll, we'll throw you up on the back and roll away downhill and you won't notice the journey at all sir

BRIEN: Alright, that's grand. Have you any nice food about you, you could give me

JOHN JOE: I don't know what goats like to eat

BRIEN: I see you have a little light lunch there in your pocket, so don't trouble yourself, I'll eat what you eat

JOHN JOE: You'll eat what I eat, that's fine. That'll save me the trouble, it will. It will save me the trouble

Time passes.

*   *   *

JOHN JOE: This is it, Fat 'Sumpter's place, where she lives with that lazy good for nothing fella, Brien

BRIEN: Go in and tell her now you have her goat for her

He goes. We hear him calling hello, and the opening of the rickety door.

BRIEN: You've very little to say for yourself for a goat that's just eaten its master

GOAT: I've your scholarly brain to do the talking for me

BRIEN: You certainly chewed up that lunch he gave us. All I got was a foul-tasting lump of bacon fat. What did you do with the meat that was on it?

GOAT: I ate it

BRIEN: Well it didn't reach your stomach

GOAT: The meaty bits get caught in my teeth sometimes, be patient, it usually works itself loose after a few days

BRIEN: You'll be laughing on the other side of your face when Fat 'Sumpter comes out here with a cleaver and rips open your belly to release me

'SUMPTER charges out from the hut.

SUMPTER: Out of my way. That's my goat, where did you find it?

JOHN JOE: The poor bloated creature was by the roadside in a ditch

SUMPTER: You didn't notice a skinny little fella asleep somewhere in the vicinity did ya?

BRIEN: 'Sumpter, 'Sumpter it's me. I'm in here!

JOHN JOE: You see it speaks just like I told you

SUMPTER: Well Lord be praised it's eaten him!

JOHN JOE: What's that?

SUMPTER: Never you mind. Now I'll tell you what, you let me have three of them beehives off your cart and you've got yourself the world's only talking goat

BRIEN: But 'Sumpter save me!

JOHN JOE: God love her she's crying out to ya!

SUMPTER: Don't be taken in, that one's always out for your sympathy, just take a stick to its belly if it gives you any trouble

JOHN JOE: It's a strange thing but it has an awful deep voice for a nanny goat

SUMPTER: And how many nanny goats' voices have you heard?

JOHN JOE: Only the one

SUMPTER: Now, those beehives. Get 'em all up on my back, that's it...

There is a lifting, a straining.

SUMPTER: ... I'll swear you're a man of the world. You've probably great plans for the poor animal?

JOHN JOE: Perhaps a world tour to start with

SUMPTER: That's swell. And what'll you do with all the money you make?

JOHN JOE: I've my eyes on a little white bungalow in Galway. All modren with the big sweep drive out in the front of it, all pebble-dashed. Beautiful sure

SUMPTER: I could tell you'd something of the cosmopolitan about your looks. Be seeing you now, may the road rise to meet you

She goes off happily laughing, with the three beehives on her back.

NARRATOR: And turning the vast expanse of her back to them 'Sumpter slouched back into the shack leaving Brien and his host, the goat, to the strictures of their new master

JOHN JOE: Come on you, get down offa that cart and let's see what kind of a goat you are, get them legs moving, and stand up straight...

*   *   *

NARRATOR: And Brien inside the goat was led away upon unknown paths leaving 'Sumpter to her life of luxury. But a mother's love is not so easily extinguished and Brien's Ma sorely missed the daily visits of her scavenging son and she came battering on 'Sumpter's door looking for him.

Time passes. Bees buzzing. BRIEN's MA pushes open the rickety door of the hut but it gets stuck on 'SUMPTER's great bulk.

MA: Brien, it's your mam, open up!

SUMPTER: (*Her voice sticky from honey.*) Stop pushing the door old woman, it's wedged on my thigh

MA: Move out of it then 'Sumpter, what're you doing lying in the dust like an old tinker, get up and greet your mother-in-law

SUMPTER: Step over me for Christ's sake if you're coming in, squeeze in by the wall there

MA: Sure you've swollen up like a balloon. What've you been eating?

SUMPTER: Only honey. That's all I've left since your son went off and left me

MA: Where is he? I wondered why he hadn't been up for the slops

SUMPTER: He's off on a world tour with a little wizened fella and a goat he reckons can talk

MA: Isn't that just like him the greedy– wait a minute. Tour of the world is it? My son wouldn't walk the length of his shoe laces without me behind him with a big stick. What have you done with him? You haven't eaten him have you?

SUMPTER: I wouldn't torment my teeth with that little bit of crackling

MA: I'll give him world tour if I catch hold of him. Is he making any money?

SUMPTER: If he is he isn't spending any of it here. Look at all I've got. Just this little spoon and this little jar of honey and a few old bees buzzing round me like a dead dog in a field

MA: You lazy trollop. You're congealed to the floor. How do you fetch in the honey?

SUMPTER: If your old carcass wasn't in the way I'd show you. I just put out my arm out of the window and scoop it in from the hive. Clever ain't I?

MA: Well necessity has provided you with genius of invention when it comes to filling your face with what's left of the planet. I'm not moving till my son is returned

*　　*　　*

NARRATOR: Meanwhile somewhere along the rolling road Brien was learning the cruel truths of the travelling life

Somewhere along the rocky road.

JOHN JOE: Get up there! Goan!

The man is driving the GOAT from behind with his stick. BRIEN and the GOAT talk in whispers.

BRIEN: Oh, o this jolting. Can't you walk a bit smoother? I'm all bruises inside here, and your ribs are sticking into me, ah ow!

GOAT: Keep quiet in there, have you no sense of adventure? We'll be famous!

BRIEN: I'll be dead from exhaustion and you'll be in the knacker's yard

GOAT: Not at all. This is the break I've been waiting for. I'm actually from a long line of entertainers. My father was with the gypsies running up and down a step ladder blowing a trumpet and a cousin on my mother's side bit the arse of King Billy himself in Phoenix Park on jubilee day

JOHN JOE: What did you say there Goatee?

GOAT: (*Bleats.*) Bleah!

JOHN JOE: Ah there's the jangling of money in that bleat. I can hear it. You'd better start practising with your jokes. We'll have the whole of Dublin splitting its sides

BRIEN: I don't know any jokes I'm telling ya

JOHN JOE: Ah you'll think of one. You don't want to disappoint all the rich English tourists at Dun Laoghaire now do ya? Give 'em a touch of the old Irish wit and they'll be throwing money at us

BRIEN: Listen old fella, I've been trying to tell you and you must believe me, I am a man inside a goat's stomach

JOHN JOE: Ah I know that. Inside every goat is a wee maneen trying to get out

BRIEN: No, no, no! Listen you old gom. My goat ate me up, and my wife, God wither the woman, sold me to you for the bee hives, and to tell you the truth this is a terrible life for me. I'm dead beat with all the walking and bumping around inside here and I'd like to go home to my little hut and sleep it all off, because I don't want to be on a world tour no more! Do you get me?

JOHN JOE: I've a good mind to take my stick to you if I thought it would do any good. But if you don't make those blighters laugh you'll be straight back home and I'll tie you up to my cart and you'll be up and down those hills like a yoyo, boy, I can tell you now

GOAT: (*Bleats.*) Bleah.

*   *   *

NARRATOR: The hard journey brought them at last to Dublin and the busy port of Dun Laoghaire in search of a worthy audience for the talking goat

The busy port of Dun Laoghaire. Horn blasts off the ships, scornful screeches of seagulls, and the chatter of the idle classes.

JOHN JOE: Ladies and Gentlemen, your lordships, gather round to hear the world's only talking goat. Not only does this goat talk away to itself in a variety of voices, male and female, but it also tells a great joke, so listen now to her and er... get your money ready... (*Aside.*) go on with your joke now

A mighty snoring emanates from the GOAT's stomach.

GOAT: Alright, em... er, well. (*Bleats.*)

JOHN JOE: What's the matter with you? Stop bleating! What's that snoring noise? Stop it! Er Ladies and Gentlemen, the world's only talking goat, she's ready for you now, just a couple of moments till I wake her up. (*Aside.*) Alright you!

He beats the GOAT with his stick.

GOAT: Come on little man inside me, wake up, wake up...

BRIEN: Don't wake me, don't wake me. I was dreaming of me mammy's place

GOAT: Now is not the time for dreaming, we're on

JOHN JOE: Ladies and Gentlemen!

ENGLISH TOURIST 1: Yah! Talking goat! Boo! Boo!

ENGLISH TOURIST 2: It's just muttering

BRIEN: Why don't you tell your joke. You're the one wants to be famous, get on with it and let me go back to sleep

GOAT: I can't I've got stage fright

BRIEN: What?

ENGLISH TOURIST 3: My good man, do you realise I have a horse that can do the Times crossword in 15 minutes. This is a terribly poor spectacle compared...

ENGLISH TOURISTS EN MASSE: Give us our money back! Boo Boo!

JOHN JOE: Wait a minute sir, I think I know what's the matter with her. (*Aside.*) If you want to get out of here alive you'd better come up with something fast, they're picking up stones

GOAT: (*Bleats in alarm.*) Bleah!

JOHN JOE: One more bleat out of you and you're sandwiches

BRIEN: Suits me fine. I'll be a free man.

GOAT: Oh will you now. And who'll carry you back home? Those thin legs of yours have a nasty surprise in store for them. Surely that great brain of yours can think of something

BRIEN: Ah gee, I'm no entertainer you know

GOAT: Ah please Brien, tell a joke for us. Think of it, we could end up on the wireless, we'd be big stars and travel around town in taxi cabs to big lunches and you could sleep all you wanted once my stomach was well padded

BRIEN: ... Alright... ahem. Well, there was these two farmers and the one says, how's business and the other says, very well, I've a million bees making honey for me in 3,000 hives. How about yourself? Well, I've three million bees. Is that a fact? You must have a great lot of hives for that load of bees. Just the one, your man says. Just the one? But it must be awful crowded in there for the poor bees. To hell with them, he says. (*Pause.*)

JOHN JOE: Is that it? Where's the punchline?

BRIEN: But that was the punchline

GOAT: I don't get it

Stones rain down on them. The crowd boo "Rubbish".

ENGLISH TOURISTS: Give us our money back

JOHN JOE: Quick, run!

BRIEN: Stop galloping, my bones are breaking

GOAT: Quit your moaning, my career's in ruins

NARRATOR: But failure in the world of entertainment brought a great thirst and the disappointed bee keeper headed directly for the renowned comfort of a Dublin pub

A busy street in the centre of Dublin. Outside a pub.

JOHN JOE: I'll just turn in here goatie, to elevate my mind. You stand there. We'll see if a few jars can't bring about my recovery

BRIEN: There he goes now, we won't see him till he lands on his nose at closing time. What kind of a clod hopper would leave a goat tied up outside of a pub in the centre of a metropolis. I'm embarrassed with folk staring, it disturbs my sleep

GOAT: You've too much of the bog-shite in you to appreciate the real cosmopolitan environment. I love it, it brings out the artist in me a lot better than the old quayside in Dun Laoghaire I can tell you. Oh yes, it's the real high life for me boy. Let 'em stare. Wait till I just get a good posture here

The GOAT struggles to his feet.

GOAT: Try and sit nicely inside me so your knees aren't sticking out and spoiling the tight drum of my glistening flanks – there's a good fella

In the background passers-by snigger and laugh.

RORY: Mangy old goat

FINBAR: Tied out by the pub door

RORY: Waiting for his glass of porter I'll bet

FINBAR: Give him a pipe

RORY: Here goatie have a smoke of this

GOAT: Thank you sir. (*Puffs.*)

BRIEN: Urgh, what is it? Have you caught on fire or what's happening?

GOAT: Yerra, I'm just having a blow on this gentleman's baccy pipe

MR SWEENEY: Look the goat's smoking away like a publican

GOAT: Isn't this the grand life

BRIEN: Blow out, blow out! I'm choking in here (*Coughs.*)

GOAT: Sit still

MRS COOMEY: Ah Rory, you've given the animal hiccoughs

FINBAR: Do a dance for us

MR HACKETT: That nanny goat has a real man's cough on her by God!

A SIMPLE PERSON: Give her some porter, poor donkey

RORY: Take a sup of this

GOAT: Don't mind if I do, good luck to you.

The GOAT slurps the drink in the glass.

MR SWEENY: Look at the old nag's tongue shooting into the glass

MR HACKETT: Hold on tight. She'll swallow the tumbler and all

GOAT smacks her lips. Gasps and sighs.

RORY: Did you enjoy that?

MRS COOMEY: I think she did, she's starting to dance

The GOAT's hooves start slowly clippity clopping on the pavement. A rudimentary fox trot develops. Music: fox trot from Ravel's L'Enfant et le santilege.

RORY: Give us a squeeze on your 'cordion Finbar

MR HACKETT: A little accompaniment maestro!

FINBAR: Won't you sing us a song to go with it Goatie?

ALL: Ha! Ha! Ha!

The GOAT sings as she dances.

GOAT: There was a fine goat
    From Kerry she came
    Her mammy was drunk
    Her daddy was lame
    But she married a gentry
    A man called Rafferty
    Who loved her then died
    And left her his property
    Which she left to the priests
    And went off on the roads
    And danced out her days
    To the sound of the fiddle
    And paid her way
    By inventing this riddle
    What's County Kildare
    And trousers between them
    In common? The both of them
    Bless us, have always Athy in them.

*The assembled crowd of RORY and FINBAR and the others dance
and whistle along cheering and laughing and tossing coins onto the
pavement.*

RORY: O well done, well done!

MR SWEENEY: Throw in your money boys!

MR HACKETT: What a great entertainer, world-class,
world-class

MRS COOMEY: Good luck to you goatie, here's money
for you

*A huge shower of ringing coins fall at the GOAT's feet. The crowd move
away, their talk fading.*

RORY: That was a great show wasn't it?

FINBAR: A very high standard indeed

RORY: You show me the Dublin goat that can sing and
dance like that...

The GOAT dances a few extra steps.

BRIEN: Alright you can stop now. I'm covered in porter
inside here

GOAT: Look at all the money I got! I told you I'd the gift

BRIEN: We'd better hide it quickly, don't the old fella take
it for himself when he emerges

GOAT: What'll we do?

BRIEN: Easy. Get that big tongue of yours onto the
pavement and swallow all the coins. I can take care
of them all in here

GOAT: Great idea

BRIEN: And maybe that'll persuade you to walk
smoother, because if you start jingling like a bishop's

purse I think you can guess whose guts he'll be slitting open. Get swallowing

Slurping is followed by coins falling into a tidy gastric pile.

NARRATOR: Content with their secret success the goat and Brien allowed themselves to be led back home in disgrace, their futures secured

*   *   *

Outside 'SUMPTER's place.

JOHN JOE: Come outside here and take a look at the goat you sold me

Sound of 'SUMPTER's bulk approaching, gulping, sweating, grunting.

SUMPTER: What is it? Out of my way. Oh it's you. Well, what's wrong with it?

JOHN JOE: Look at it

A loud snoring from the bowels of the GOAT.

Talking goat, you said. Well I've been halfways around the world and all I've heard from it is complaining and now it has retreated entirely into snoring even when it's awake and I can't get a word out of it

SUMPTER: Well I don't know, give it a poke

JOHN JOE: I've poked it, I could poke it till Christmas, look

He pokes. The GOAT bleats "Bleah".

I don't want it. I thought I'd make a load of money but this donkey of a goat isn't at all the thing for the sophisticated audiences you find where I've been. Sure, they've seen it all. Now I'm a ruined man. I'm exhausted. Didn't I have to carry the blasted animal the last thirty miles, there's no life in it at all

SUMPTER: Well, I don't want it back if that's what you're driving at

JOHN JOE: Ah please missus, God help me I haven't the strength to feed and carry the monstrous stomach developing on it. It's bigger every day and I'm only a poor old fella (*Cries.*)

SUMPTER: You're too late. I can't look after it. I'm too fat now to bend down and hit it

JOHN JOE: But you could kick it with one of the fine big legs you have on you

SUMPTER: I'll not go waving my legs around for no goat mister

JOHN JOE: Or you could sit on it. You see it needs the discipline I can't provide

SUMPTER: I can't say I don't pity your miserable plight so I'll tell you what. See that heap of clothes in the mud underneath my window? Well that, believe it or not, is the proud mother of a son who's gone off and left us all to wait until he returned from his travels. I'll call her, maybe she can help you. Hey old mother, swivel your eye sockets round in this direction a moment. We've a thing for you

MA: What is it, Fat 'Sumpter?

JOHN JOE: Pleasant day Mrs!

SUMPTER: Now listen to me. We have a distended stomach on legs no-one wants and I was thinking it would be great company for you till Brien turns up with his crock of gold. Sure, you'll hardly recognise the difference

MA: What is the creature? Forgive me sir I'm blind with searching the horizon for my lost son. The strain of trying to pick out his pitiful physique coming along the road has worn my eyeballs down to the handles

JOHN JOE: It's only a goat but the great thing is with it that you're not missing much not getting the sight of it. And it won't bother you for it hardly moves all day

MA: Alright. I'll take it off your hands for you

JOHN JOE: I'd be most grateful.

MA: Don't you want nothing for your goat?

JOHN JOE: No, I'm well shot of it. I'll just be off now to my little houseen over the hill on my own to my old bees. I can just hear them buzzing, by Jesus, it will be a peaceful easy life, it will, a peaceful easy life... (*He wanders away.*)

MA: (*With a wild cackle.*) I tricked him! I tricked him! I'm not as blind as all that. Goodbye 'Sumpter, and good luck to you girlie. Heh, heh!

She drives the GOAT with its snoring belly.

MA: Go on up that hill, home goatee. Get them little legs moving, don't they be after us. And stop that gastric snoring son, you don't fool me. What a genius you are Brien with the hitch-hiking. Isn't it just like you to hoodwink the unsuspecting into transporting you across country with all your money. We'll be safe home in a few minutes and we'll unload all the booty. Was it a lot of money you made son? I'll bet it was. They all told me you was good for nothing but I knew alright. Now I've got my eye on one of them new white bungalows in Galway, with the pebbledash and all modren inside.

The snoring continues as the GOAT stumbles along bleating occasionally.

NARRATOR: But dreams, like wakefulness have their disappointments, usually the unhappy conjunction of the two. Brien was woken by a familiar voice. He was once again by the roadside, still in his ditch

By the roadside again.

SUMPTER: Brien, Brien wake up. God rot your slothful bones

BRIEN: (*Sleepily.*) Ah 'Sumpter...

SUMPTER: Have you been here all this while, I thought I told you, go up to the beehive man and sell the goat. Where are your shoes?

BRIEN: The goat has eaten them, but don't worry

SUMPTER: I'll be a lot less worried boy when I see you disappearing over that hill

BRIEN: There's no need. I'll show you

SUMPTER: What are you doing? Stop it!

BRIEN strains as he lifts up the GOAT. Urgent bleating.

SUMPTER: Put the goat down. You'll destroy the last bit of life that's left in it

BRIEN: ... It just needs a good shake about, wait till I get it upside down, there we are (*Shakes.*)

SUMPTER: What are you doing you simple creature! Stop it!

Wild bleating as he shakes the GOAT.

BRIEN: I'm trying... to get... the money... out... of the goat's... stomach. Get your fat little hands into the money bag position and hold still

SUMPTER: Stop it, stop it!

Wild bleating.

NARRATOR: And so it was that Lazy Brien made his
fortune without having to leave the ditch at the bottom
of the lane. And without wearing himself thin with travel
and ambition, as is the case with so many of the young
men going nowadays.

The End.